CHAUCER

THE PROLOGUE TO
THE CANTERBURY TALES

Chaucer

The Prologue to the Canterbury Tales

EDITED BY

R. T. DAVIES M.A. Oxon.

Lecturer in English Literature
in the University of Liverpool

Nelson

Thomas Nelson and Sons Ltd
Nelson House Mayfield Road
Walton-on-Thames Surrey
KT12 5PL UK

Nelson Blackie
Wester Cleddens Road
Bishopbriggs
Glasgow
G64 2NZ UK

Thomas Nelson Australia
102 Dodds Street
South Melbourne
Victoria 3205 Australia

Nelson Canada
1120 Birchmount Road
Scarborough Ontario
M1K 5G4 Canada

© Thomas Nelson and Sons Ltd 1987

First published by George G. Harrap and Co. Ltd 1953
ISBN 0-245-52895-4

This edition published by Thomas Nelson and Sons Ltd 1987

I(T)P Thomas Nelson is an International
       Thomson Publishing Company

I(T)P is used under licence

ISBN 0-17-444107-X
NPN 9 8

Printed in Singapore

CONTENTS

THE PILGRIMS

References to notes on the individual pilgrims are shown in capital letters as follows:

ABBREVIATIONS USED IN THIS EDITION

adj., adjective
adv., adverb
auxil., auxiliary
b., born
c. (*circa*), about
cf., compare
conj., conjunction
dat., dative
exclam., exclamation
fig., figurative
Fr., French
gen., genitive
imp., imperative
impers., impersonal
inf., infinitive
It., Italian
l(l)., line(s)
L., Latin
lit., literally
M.E., Middle English
n., noun
O.E., Old English
orig., originally

pl., plural
p.p., past participle
pr., present
prep., preposition
pron., pronoun
prp., present participle
pt., preterite
q.v. (*quod vide*), which see
rel., relative
refl., reflexive
s., singular
subj., subjunctive
v., verb infinitive

If no person is given with
tense and number of a
verb, the third person is to
be understood.
In line references to the *Can-
terbury Tales* the letters
refer to the groupings of
the tales in the editions of
Furnivall and Skeat.

INTRODUCTION

Chaucer's Life

CHAUCER'S relations on his father's side were prosperous wholesale wine-merchants and customs officials. They lived at Ipswich, then a large port on the river Orwell.[1] Geoffrey himself did not become a merchant but, when we first hear of him in 1357, was in the household of the Countess of Ulster, wife of Lionel, third son of Edward III, the reigning king. He was probably a page; and thus began his career as a courtier, for he is referred to in 1367 as a "yeoman" and later as a "squire," now in the king's own service.[2]

As a squire Chaucer may have had duties as various as making beds or keeping the king's money, bearing messages to foreign courts or serving at the royal table. He travelled as a diplomat on the Continent, twice, at least, visiting Italy, though there is no evidence that he there or in France met any poets. But the cultures of France and England were then so similar that a poet at the English court, especially since the queen was from Hainaut, had no need to travel to become familiar with French poetry. His wife, Philippa, whom he married about 1366 and of whom no more is heard after 1387, was one of the ladies attending Queen Philippa, and she may have come herself with the queen from Hainaut.

Like the squire of the Prologue, he went to war against France; he was taken prisoner and ransomed in 1360,

[1] *Cf.* THE MERCHANT.
[2] See THE YEOMAN and SQUIRE.

probably at this time in his late teens. We know nothing certain about his education. It has been suggested on reasonable evidence that the years between 1360 and 1367, about which we know nothing, were spent in part at the Inner Temple studying law and perhaps other subjects too.[1]

Chaucer's income was chiefly derived from patrons; he received annuities from Edward III and Richard II as an officer of their households, and also, for services done, from John of Gaunt, the second son of Edward and uncle to Richard. But he earned further money from various government posts. His average annual income from all sources was about that of an Assistant Secretary in the British Civil Service to-day, but by no means so secure, depending as much on others' favour as his own efficiency; and though there is no sign that Chaucer was ever destitute, there are suggestions of one or two tight financial corners.

He was Controller of the Customs on Wool and Hides in the port of London from 1374 to 1386, and Controller of the Petty Customs from 1382 to 1386. From 1389 to 1391 he was Clerk of the King's Works at Westminster, the Tower of London, Eltham, Shene, and many other places, organizing building programmes and keeping meticulous inventories of ladles and frying-pans. In his last years he was a 'forester' or official administering a great royal estate at North Petherton in Somerset.[2]

Chaucer was made a J.P. for Kent in 1385, and an M.P. for that county in 1386. He returned to London, however, not long before he died, and was buried in 1400 in Westminster Abbey. He had leased a house quite near the Abbey after successfully petitioning King Henry IV, who deposed Richard II in 1399, to continue his pension—the

[1] *Cf.* A MAUNCIPLE.
[2] *Cf.* THE YEOMAN.

last and perhaps most diplomatic piece of business done by a reasonably successful civil servant and courtier.

Chaucer's Work

It may have been Chaucer's wish for more time at his literary work that led to his leaving the post of Controller of Customs in 1386, soon after which he is generally supposed to have been writing the *Canterbury Tales*. When he became a government official, writing would appear to have been an occupation for his spare time. The *House of Fame*,[1] which describes with unprecedented dexterity and life how Jove's eagle carried a bewildered Chaucer through the heavens, refers to the poet's going home after he has totted up his accounts in the office, there to read himself silly in solitude; and the eagle says that he made his head ache at night by composing love poems, though himself not a lover. If the writing of love poetry, elaborately eloquent and concerned with intense and fine feelings, was the spare-time pursuit of a civil servant, the Trollope of his day, it was also an accomplishment desirable in a medieval courtier; and several of Chaucer's formal lover's complaints survive.

Their poise and courtliness may be compared with that of the earlier love poetry of France and Italy, and their expansiveness and magniloquence, though owing nothing, in all probability, directly to Dante, the first great Italian poet, have something of the same effect as the 'high' style which he taught.[2] There had been fine lyric poetry written in English before Chaucer's day, but none so close in

[1] Probably written in the earlier part of his career as Controller of Customs, before he had appointed a deputy: probably not long after 1374.
[2] In his *De Vulgari Eloquentia*.

language and feeling to other European verse. It is of such poetry as this in English that Chaucer is the father, and his achievement was unrivalled until the sonnets and dignified stanzas of Sidney, Spenser, and Shakespeare.

He also wrote longer poems concerning love, the *Parliament of Birds*, the *Book of the Duchess*, and the *Legend of Good Women*.[1] These are influenced by the 'dream-allegory,' which was first used in the *Roman de la Rose*, a thirteenth-century French poem which Chaucer himself translated. In such poems the poet falls asleep, often disturbed by love, and the dream which follows and which makes the body of the poem is allegorical. The *Legend of Good Women* extravagantly praises women who were noble in love, and in this it follows the French romantic tradition; but these lives of Cupid's saints are to be given, says the poem, to the English queen at 'Eltham or at Shene' and were, perhaps, immediately occasioned by the demands of the ladies of the English court. The poem is imposed as a penance, partly for his having written the story of how a lady, Criseyde, was unfaithful to her lover Troilus.

Troilus and Criseyde,[2] Chaucer's most ambitious love poem, and a work perhaps greater than the *Canterbury Tales*—though the fact that the first is finished, and the second is not, makes it hard to judge fairly—is a tragedy describing how Troilus passed "Fro wo to wele and after out of joye." Based on a version of the story by Boccaccio, it is even more medieval in form and sentiment than

[1] *Parliament of Birds* has not been dated conclusively, but is generally dated about 1382. *Book of the Duchess*, written soon after the death in 1369 of Blanche, Duchess of Lancaster, the occasion of the poem. *Legend of Good Women* mentions *Troilus and Criseyde*, *House of Fame*, and *Parliament of Birds*, and shows revision: 1386(?)–1395(?)

[2] Written 1385(?)–86(?)—at least before Thomas Usk's *Testament of Love*, which shows familiarity with it and was probably written in 1387.

its Italian original; yet its subtlety in delineation of character links it with the modern novel, and its concern with human destiny and free will gives it that philosophical seriousness that has always been an element in the greatest English poetry.

In this Chaucer was doubtless influenced by Dante, but more especially he presented in a speaking picture the philosophy expressed in the *De Consolatione Philosophiæ* of Boethius, an Italian imprisoned in the early sixth century by the barbarians overthrowing the Roman Empire. It concerns the injustice of the world, the misfortunes of good men, and life's cruel instability. It teaches that it is foolish to trust in the world: the aim should be not possession of good fortune but of oneself. Chaucer translated this work. Like the *Roman de la Rose*, it was of the utmost importance in shaping his imagination; and like the *Retraction* at the end of the *Canterbury Tales*, the high seriousness of *Troilus and Criseyde*, and the sheer volume of his rhetorical love-poetry, it must be remembered as a guard against assessing Chaucer's literary personality from the *Canterbury Tales* alone.

Chaucer and Rhetoric

Elaborate eloquence was felt to be especially attractive in the Middle Ages. Then the cultivated man liked rhetoric. For us rhetoric means very often 'mere words,' and is associated with hollowness and deception. But though this was also sometimes true in the Middle Ages, the art of rhetoric was then, in general, appreciated as the proper instrument for persuading men seriously to the truth, and a noble way to give pleasure.

The art was taught in the universities and by several systematic text-books. Chaucer refers, though jokingly, to the author of one of them, Geoffrey de Vinsauf (who lived at the end of the twelfth century), in the Nun's Priest's Tale. These text-books took much from the rhetorical treatises of the ancient world, especially from Cicero's *De Inventione* and from a work wrongly attributed to him, *De Rhetorica ad Herrenium*. In Cicero's time such rhetoric was primarily practised by pleaders in the law-courts, but in the Middle Ages its methods were applied to the composition of official, and therefore dignified, letters, and of poetry with a noble subject.

It is natural to use language as persuasively and pleasurably as possible, and to feel certain expressions more appropriate on some occasions than on others. Such 'rhetoric' we all use. When we say, "You could have heard a pin drop," rather than, "There was complete silence," we are using rhetoric. The direct statement is insufficiently powerful, and so we evoke our meaning through a startling picture. We do the same in saying, "Dead as a door-nail," but we also add the power of sound in impressing the picture by alliteration.

Our text-books, however, systematize and elaborate this natural practice and turn it into an art which we can learn. Thus we study 'figures of speech' and learn, for example, that the persuasive figure used in "Dead as a door-nail" is called a 'simile.' We also find more elaborate rhetorical devices which it is unlikely we should have used spontaneously, such as 'chiasmus'—the neatly reversed word order in the biblical "I cannot dig, to beg I am ashamed," where pattern incises the idea and decorates it.

We find also that some expressions are more appropriate on some occasions than on others. In church, for example, we hear appropriately dignified language that would be unbearably pompous in the living-room. There are also certain proprieties in the conduct of speech-days and legal cases which we accept, and even enjoy, just as scouts and soldiers often practise ceremonial which is not only appropriate but can also be fun.

Thus, when decorum requires it and to give pleasure to those who enjoy dignified formalities, Chaucer will practise a 'figure' of rhetoric called *exclamatio*, a formal 'exclamation' of grief or reproach. In *Troilus and Criseyde* Troilus stands before the palace of Criseyde, now empty because she has deserted it and him, and cries,

> O paleis desolat,
> O hous of houses whilo best yhight, [called]
> O paleis empty and disconsolat,
> O thow lanterne of whiche queint [put out] is the light.

He continues for fourteen lines, varying his descriptions of the house, but using always the same formula. Thus also the beginning of the Prologue is not a simple, direct statement of time and place, but an elaborate series of circumlocutions. Chaucer here is deliberately not calling a spade a spade. He is practising the learned art of rhetoric.

And it was not Chaucer's vigorous, colloquial, and racy style for which he was famous among his poetical successors, but his rhetorical. Few things could better demonstrate the change in taste between their day and ours. His follower, Hoccleve, for example, compared him with Cicero, the great Roman rhetorician, and lamented that Chaucer's death had deprived England

> . . . the swetnesse
> Of rethoric: for unto Tullius
> Was never man so like amonges us.

Such praise kept company with reverence for the philosophy of Chaucer's poetry, and one poet called him "superlative . . . in moralitee and eloquence ornate." It is implied that serious *sentence* (see Glossary) was appropriately accompanied by a 'high' style, which made the teaching delightful.

Chaucer has at least two styles, therefore, and though we often find that we prefer the one whereas his immediate successors preferred the other, neither can be ignored. He is often simple and colloquial, but on other occasions elaborate and lofty. Sometimes he is nearer Wordsworth of many "Lyrical Ballads," sometimes Milton of *Paradise Lost*.

The Canterbury Tales

Chaucer's most popular work, the *Canterbury Tales*, set out to be a dramatic sequence of stories in prose and verse. To enliven a pilgrimage to Canterbury, a group of "sondry folk" agree to tell four stories each on the way, two going and two coming back, the whole entertainment to be organized by the keeper of the inn from which they set out.

But Chaucer appears never to have completed this ambitious project. No pilgrim except the author himself tells more than one story, seven tell none at all (namely, the five Townsmen, the Yeoman, and the Ploughman), and two tales (those of the Cook and Squire) are left unfinished. In the introduction to the tale of the Parish Priest, the Host calls for his tale, saying that "everyman, save thou, hath toold his tale," and adds that only one tale remains to be told to fulfil the Host's "decree." This seems to imply that Chaucer's intention is altered, and that only one tale is expected of each pilgrim; but not even this modified scheme has come down to us complete.

In l. 24 of the Prologue Chaucer says that "fully twenty-nine" pilgrims were at the Tabard. He describes, however, only twenty-seven, and in addition mentions three priests attendant, presumably, on the Lady Prioress. The numbers will not tally, either with or without these three. It may be that "fully" is intended to smooth over the discrepancy, but it is more likely that it shows typical casualness.

It has been suggested that the reference to three priests was not made by Chaucer at all but by an editor, to fill up l. 164, which the author had left unfinished, intending to continue it by describing the character of the Nun Chaplain. No manuscript has any different version of the line, so that the correction, if such it is, must have been made very early. Two points arise from this. First, that it is often difficult to distinguish between corrections made by Chaucer and those made by later hands. In this case there is no proof either way. Secondly, that the variations in the text of the many manuscripts—there are fifty-eight in which the Tales are relatively complete—are only to be explained by the probability that when Chaucer died he left the work in a number of disordered papers, probably not all in one place, some the revisions of others not yet destroyed, and all quite unready for publication as a finished whole. It is likely that some separate tales had circulated among his friends while he was alive, and he may have read some aloud to an audience; but it was not until after his death that friends, eager for more of what they had sampled, and commercial copyists of manuscripts, like the publishers of the day, made several attempts at finding Chaucer's intended text and order of tales, and, editing away some of the inconsistencies and omissions, produced versions of the work varying in a few major and many minor respects.

The extant stories are as diverse as the characters who tell them. The Knight's Tale is of love and battle, long, richly coloured, and noble; the Miller's Tale is fast, vulgar, boisterous with racy detail and comedy; the Prioress's Tale is well-made, short, pious, with appropriate tender sentiments; satire on displays of learning and the misuse of elaborate rhetoric in poetry is built by the Nun's Priest about a sharp, bright fable of the cockerel who would not take his wife's advice; and the Parish Priest preaches a sermon of solemn warning about the seven mortal sins. Often the tales are obviously appropriate to their tellers, but this could hardly be said of the tales of the Manciple, or Serjeant at Law.

There had been comparable collections of stories[1] before Chaucer, but none is given organic unity by the natural drama of a pilgrimage and its current entertainment. As the pilgrims ride along quarrels appear between some of them, for example, between the Miller and the Reeve, and their tales are told at each other's expense. Perhaps further drama was intended in a discussion from diverse points of view of the relationship of love and marriage, a theme that had always attracted Chaucer. This is suggested by a certain likeness between the subjects of some tales, for example, those of the Wife of Bath, the Merchant, and the Franklin. But this can have been, at the most, only part of his intention, and unexpressed at that.

But the general diversity of the tales was, plainly, planned Introducing the Miller's Tale, Chaucer refers to at least three varieties, stories of common people, pseudo-historical stories about the manners of gentle-folk, and pious and moral tales. He apologizes to his well-bred readers for the first, and tells them to turn the pages till they find the second. At this point he defends the vulgar subject-matter of the Miller's and Reeve's Tales, just as at ll. 725–742 of the Prologue he defends his use of vulgar language on the grounds that he must not be untrue to his art. He must

---

[1] Two, particularly, in Italian: Boccaccio's *Decameron* and Sercambi's *Novelle*. There is no reason to believe that Chaucer knew them.

"report" what was told accurately. The man who "reports" ill-breeding is not himself necessarily ill-bred.[1]

Though it is clear that the author enjoys his characters and situations, high and low, moral and immoral, we are bidden not to make "earnest of game." We are bidden not to judge of the morals and proprieties by which Chaucer regulated his everyday life from this practice of what Keats called "negative capability." And, indeed, in the retraction following the Parson's Tale, which has every appearance of being written to make an earlier end to the sequence than was at first intended, Chaucer deliberately revokes all those tales that "sownen into synne." For his soul's health he finally renounced works in which he had shown his chief strength as an artist.[2] In final "earnest" he renounced the "game."

The Prologue

Like most authors in the Middle Ages when books were few, Chaucer wrote rather to be listened to than to be read, and his style was affected by the exigencies of public recitation. Thus he sounds sometimes more like a preacher or lecturer than a poet, making his transitions from one point to another very clear—

> But for to tellen yow of his array, (73)
> But therof nedeth nat to speke as nowthe. (462.)

—and explaining anything that is likely not to be under-

---

[1] *Cf.* same excuse in *Roman de la Rose*, ll. 15159 ff., and by Boccaccio in the *Conclusione dell' Autore* of the *Decameron*.

[2] Many medieval authors feared eventually that they had offended God, and quieted their consciences in the same way by retracting what they had written.

stood on a first hearing; for example, the comparison of an undisciplined Monk

> ... til a fish that is waterlees;

which may be obscure, and is explained thus:

> This is to seyn, a monk out of his cloistre. (180–181.)

To reduce strain on the listener the sense is diluted by using conventional phrases—often doublets—which demand no strenuous or subtle thought, for example, "war and wis" (309), "faire and fetisly" (124 and 273), and by almost meaningless tags such as "for the nonis" (523); while the general directness and concreteness of the Prologue meet the aural need for clarity and simplicity, and are anyway the normal virtues of a good *raconteur*.

The vocabulary, syntax, and tone of the Prologue are, on the whole, colloquial. Narrative easily slides into dialogue (*cf.* l. 828), and such vigorous commonplaces as "nat worth an oystre" (182) and he cared not "a pulled hen" (177) suggest an emphatic conversation.

The brief introduction to the Prologue is in a more elaborate and lofty vein not to be repeated (see note, ll. 1–12), but at l. 19 Chaucer leans slightly forward and engages his listening audience with well-bred garrulity. His next sentence (19–28) runs through nine lines, overflowing from one to another, the parts of it loosely jointed, the syntax unelaborate, the easy vocabulary and the simplicity of his reference offering no impediment to his infectious sprightliness. It is a typically bustling beginning. But Chaucer does not shout or thump the table. He talks nimbly but with restraint. His quiet irony is that of one tolerant and assured, so that there are no hysterics and no *gaucherie*.

Thus in the lines,

Discreet he was, and of greet reverence:
He semed swich, hise wordes weren so wise. (312–313.)

there is an easy and familiar sophistication. These lines are
not clipped and tightened and calculated to the last letter as
they would be in the satires of Pope.

The Prologue is characterized by a sort of continence.
About it there is no suspicion of affectation, and there is no
straining after effects. Thus in the lines,

Hise eyen stepe and rollinge in his heed,
That stemed as a forneis of a leed; (201–202)

the concrete visual simile is typical, but it is exceptional for
its slight extravagance. Puns are rare and almost accidental.
There are no brilliant and obscure conceits. The style is
plain. This poetry, a poetry that is almost prose, often
seems to us no poetry at all, for it has none of those half-
tones in its imagery, none of those vaguely evocative words
which abound in Shakespeare, Keats, or Mr T. S. Eliot, no
remote allusions, hardly a metaphor, none of the splendid
hyperbole of the Elizabethan stage.

Syntactical difficulties are rare in Chaucer,[1] for, unlike
the Elizabethan dramatists, he is rarely in a hurry, never
has to cram a world of tragic passion into the brief two
hours' traffic of a stage, telescoping images and starting to
say a second thing before finishing the first.

Chaucer's imagery is simple, direct, and concrete, so that
the lines,

Hise eyen twinkled in his heed aright
As doon the sterres in the frosty night, (267–268)

are precise and unsuggestive. Each word is clear and bright

[1] See note ll. 12–14 and *cf.* 366–368. Any obscurity in ll. 351–352
is due to the action not of a poetic mind, but of one that generally
cared less about logic in written language than we do. The difficulties
of ll. 173–176 and 396–397 are in a different category: see notes to
those lines.

like new; there is no patina of age about it. Somehow, though these words had been used for centuries before, the language seems in its youth.

All of his descriptions are of a piece with this. The portrait of the Squire is made from so ordinary an adverb as *wel*, unselfconsciously repeated, from the adjective *fresshe*, so unashamedly conventional when used of flowers, from the unmodified clear colours 'white' and 'red,' the unpretentious simile, "like a meadow," and a plain and simple statement of his accomplishments, singing, dancing, and writing.

It is for this same freshness that the first lines of the Prologue are famous. Yet they are full of echoes from earlier literature in English and other languages, and a contemporary reader would take pleasure in their very familiarity. The ideas, though not necessarily the individual words, have well-known literary associations. Our modern respect for originality is shocked by such plagiarism, but few medieval poets were primarily concerned with novelty of idea. With quiet assurance Chaucer takes old and well-worn images in ll. 496–506 and is content to present them again in easy couplets, pointed and a little graced by anti-thesis and balance.

Indeed, despite the general sobriety of the Prologue, long before those masters of polished verse satire, Pope and Dryden, Chaucer had incidentally perfected for his more amiable ends many of their own satirical devices. Chaucer's descriptions often stiffen locally into balanced lines which are terse and forceful. Antithesis, alliteration, and a rhythm in which, though the line is generally deca-syllabic, there are four and not five weighted syllables or accents, give a formal sharpness to such lines as,

His hors weren goode, but he was nat gay; (74)
That firste he wroghte, and afterward he taughte. (497.)

But such lines are not elegant like Pope's. They are like the style of the Clerk of Oxford,

> ... short and quik and ful of hy sentence. (306.)

In the century after he wrote, Caxton[1] used just the terms Chaucer used of the Clerk of Chaucer's style as a whole— "eschewyng prolyxyte"—and one of Chaucer's French contemporaries, the poet Deschamps, called him, amongst other things, "concise in speech."

On the other hand, Chaucer delights in a lengthy display of learning, as when he describes the medical prowess of the Physician, and in a long list of names—for example, the Physician's medical authorities, or the battles in which the Knight has fought. He relishes the sound as well as the significance of the many ointments that had failed to defeat the Summoner's face, and now and then multiplies words for the learned joy of it; for example,

> Were it by aventure, or sort, or cas. (844.)
> By foreward and by composicioun. (848.)

These features are the more extravagant variations in a work generally more sober and reticent, but as regards characters and style always quietly diversified.

II

Though Chaucer probably had no model for the series of character descriptions that has made the Prologue famous, he was not the first medieval writer to create characters in compact paragraphs of concrete detail. They are to be found, for example, some more, some less like, and with important differences, in the *Roman de la Rose*. In this

---

[1] Proem to the second edition of *The Canterbury Tales*. Chaucer learnt balance and antithesis from Ovid and medieval French poets who had also learnt from him.

allegory, abstractions such as Covetousness, Old Age, and
Idleness are given body and blood, and made into persons,
with features described in that visualized detail at which
Chaucer excels, and with dispositions whose characteris-
tics are, of course, those of the abstraction they represent.
Chaucer's version of the lady Idleness in the *Romaunt* fore-
shadows his description of the lady Prioress, and he has
made the homely simile in the second line even more
concrete and picturesque than the original by adding
"scoured newe."

> Hir heer was as yelowe of hewe
> As ony basin scoured newe;
> Hir flesh tendre as is a chike,
> With bente browis smothe and slyke; [sleek]
> And by mesure [proportionately] large were
> The opening of hir yen [eyes] clere;
> Hir nose of good proporcioun,
> Hir yen grey as is a faucoun,
> With swete breth and wel savoured;
> Hir face whit and wel coloured
> With litel mouth and round to see . . .
> Fro Jerusalem unto Burgoyne
> Ther nis a fairer necke, iwis,
> To fele how smothe and softe it is; . . .
> And she hadde on a cote of grene
> Of cloth of Gaunt; withouten wene,
> Wel semide by hir apparaile
> She was not wont to gret travaile.
> For whan she cempt [combed] was fetisely,
> And wel arayed and richely,
> Thanne had she don al hir journee; [day's work]
> For merye and wel bigoon [joyous] was she.
>
> (539-549, 554-556, 573-580.)

Notice also that like Chaucer's characters there is none
better than this lady: none has a fairer neck than she. It is
the same simple exaggeration as occurs in fairy stories. For
this conventional device Chaucer has a peculiar fondness.

Character-sketches like Chaucer's are also found in the

popular moral literature of the Middle Ages, in which par-
ticular sins such as pride or envy are made real to the sinner
in miniature 'speaking pictures' of real proud or envious
men. Text-books of the art of writing taught how to
describe characters feature by feature. But such formal
descriptions as those they taught are lifeless; such 'speaking
pictures' of sin in religious literature, generally grotesquely
simple and specialized; and such personified abstractions in
allegorical verse, conspicuously unshaped and desultory,
compared with Chaucer's novel achievement in a never-
theless established field.[1]

The likeness, however, between Chaucer and some
earlier writers in method and detail suggests that some of
Chaucer's characters may not be simply a direct image of
life, but one at least filtered through established literary
modes. It suggests, for example, that to some extent he
saw the hypocrisy of actual Pardoners and Friars in terms
of the hypocrisy described in detail in the *Roman de la
Rose*.[2] In the same way it is likely that he created the Reeve
and the Franklin partly in terms of the psychology of his
day, for he calls them specifically 'choleric' and 'sanguine'
men, and the characters to be expected of both were often
described in detail in medieval text-books.

That the Friar and the Franklin are not, however, more
than a little indebted to such sources is one of the reasons
why they are exuberantly alive and not the mere dead letter
of literary types. There is ample evidence that many of
Chaucer's characters are accurate reproductions of real
corruption, real merriment, and real gentility, and many of
their features can be paralleled in the less entertaining and
more didactic writings of his contemporaries,[3] which are,
perhaps, a plainer record of the times.

[1] See THE FRIAR.   [2] See THE FRIAR.
[3] See THE PARSON, SERJEANT AT LAW, and MERCHANT.

This, while supporting our sense that they are drawn
from life, weakens the likelihood that they are the portraits
of actual persons. Suspicion that they may be is aroused
by Chaucer's specific references; for example, to the
Friar's name as "Huberd" (269), to the Shipman's boat
as "Maudelaine" (410) and, suggestively, to his home,
"for aught I woot," as "Dertemouthe" (389).[1] Moreover
it sometimes happens that what appears a general allusion
seems to gain in clarity and sharpness if it can be taken as a
personal one.[2]

In the Cook's Prologue the Host is called "Herry
Bailly," and in the general Prologue his inn is the "Tabard"
at "Southwerk" (20). There is good evidence of the
existence of an inn-keeper of that name in Southwark at
least in 1380–81, but his inn is not named. In the Cook's
Prologue the Cook is said to be "of London" and calls
himself "Hogge of Ware." References to an actual "Roger
Ware of London, Cooke," (Hogge is a nickname for
"Roger") are found in records of Chaucer's day. There
was a ship called the "Maudelayne" sailing from Dart-
mouth in the late fourteenth century, but attempts to
identify the known masters with the shipman himself are
purely speculative and contradictory. Despite Chaucer's
provocative references and the suggestive live individual-
ity of his characters, no personal identification has yet been
conclusively proved.

III

Though Chaucer's imagery is not oblique, his irony is;
though his syntax is commonly simple, several of his
character-descriptions are composed of ambiguities and
fine shades of meaning; though his language is direct, his

---

[1] Cf. also ll. 284, 606–607, 620, and see A MAUNCIPLE.
[2] See note, ll. 124–152.

references are frequently elusive. It it extremely difficult to sense exactly the character of the Prioress, or the extent and quality of the irony intended by the Merchant's being in debt.

The virtue of this uncertainty of effect is pre-eminent in the creation of a character herself so intangible and ambivalent as the Prioress, or as Criseyde in Chaucer's long love poem. Uncertainty about them as people gratifies a sophisticated taste for the complex and difficult (a taste also gratified by the complexity and difficulty of Elizabethan dramatic verse) and is at the same time just what one feels about some actual human beings in the actual world. To catch the likeness of such a woman as the Prioress lies in the power of the greatest only. Chaucer has done it by reticence in presentation as well as by creative sympathy. He deliberately says too little. He makes no explanatory comments. He understates.

He often leaves his irony equally unsignposted: perhaps when he read the poetry aloud he emphasized an ironic intention by the tone of his voice or the curl of his lip.

> For unto swich a worthy man as he
> Acorded nat, as by his facultee,
> To have with sike lazars aqueintaunce.
> It is nat honeste, it may nat avaunce,
> For to deelen with no swich poraille,
> But al with riche and selleres of vitaille.
>
> (243–248.)

This is reticent as well as subtle. His professed agreement with the Monk's arguments against the cloistered life is even more so:

> And I seide, his opinioun was good. (183.)

The strength of such comic irony is in the seriousness of it. Chaucer keeps his face quite straight. It is also its weakness, because there is a chance that the irony will escape us altogether, or, on the other hand, that we shall sense irony like a ghost in a graveyard where actually there is none at all. Thus many have thought Chaucer at his most bitterly ironic in his remarks on the power of the keys in the character of the Summoner (659–662), whereas, all things considered, it is more likely that the remarks are direct and simple.

Uncertainty of effect sometimes derives from Chaucer's otherwise agreeably casual and desultory manner. One may speculate how much this manner is one of design. In describing several characters, however, in the Prologue Chaucer passes with no apparent sense of incongruity from facial details to the state of the soul, from mention of brains to mention of boots. The Franklin's mere knife and pouch are, for example, sandwiched between the dignity of his offices (355–360), and the effect is that, in the character before us, a dagger and the government service are of equal value. If, then, on some uncommon occasion Chaucer intends adjacent details to be unequal and wishes, through that incongruity, to make us laugh, it is difficult to know that he does so. There is scarcely likely to be doubt of the mischievous wit which has juxtaposed the horror of the Cook's disease and the deliciousness of his cooking (384–387), but where the incongruity is less obvious there is danger of uncertainty.

Thus Chaucer, as a rule, does not build up to his ironical remarks. They happen as if by accident, just as in the middle of a serious portrayal of the Clerk of Oxford he executes a quite independent flourish by punning on the word 'philosopher' (297–298), and then continues once more in the serious vein.

It is not true, however, that all the characters are described casually. The character of the Physician, for example, is neatly finished off with a pun on 'gold,' and

several others are built in varying degrees to simple plans.[1]
But Chaucer had no formula for the making of a character
except that very elastic one which he mentions in ll. 37–41,
and of which he occasionally reminds us (*cf*. ll. 73 and 330).

> Me thinketh it acordaunt to resoun
> To telle yow al the condicioun
> Of ech of hem, so as it semed me,
> And whiche they were, and of what degree,
> And eek in what array that they were inne:

There are several passages[2] of builded satire, in which a
succession of ironies is contrived or in which Chaucer
abandons the attitude more normal in the Prologue of one
conversing with merely desultory brilliance. In the charac-
ter of the Friar (221–232) ten lines lead up to the climactic
irony of

> Therfore instede of wepinge and preyeres
> Men moote yeve silver to the poure freres.

The diversity of Chaucer's method and attitude, and of
the uses to which he puts his characters for our entertain-
ment, is unmistakably shown by comparing the descrip-
tions of the Parish Priest, Miller, Prioress, and Manciple.
The first is treated seriously and directly without irony or
obliqueness of any sort, except that it is plainly implied
that any parish priest who is not like this ideal one is
wrong. This Priest is unlike his wicked fellows:

> He sette nat his benefice to hire,
> And leet his sheepe encombred in the mire.
>
> (507–508.)

Not one physical feature of the Priest is mentioned, but
three-quarters of the lines on the Miller are devoted to his
appearance. The one is almost entirely a sober list of a

---

[1] *Cf.* THE KNIGHT, FRANKLIN, and SUMMONER.
[2] *Cf.* also ll. 184–189 and 573–586.

priest's moral virtues; the other is one of the Prologue's most racy and colourful caricatures. There are none of Chaucer's short, vivid, homely similes in the first, whereas the second has four such: the Miller's beard is red as a sow or fox, wide like a spade, and his mouth is like a great furnace. Like the description of the Priest, however, that of the Miller is direct—except for the oblique and puzzling

And yet he haddè a thombe of gold, pardee. (563.)

But the Prioress is different again, a portrait full of half-lights, subtleties, and delicate hints. It is not implied that she is wrong or right in being what she is, but at the same time the opportunity is not lost of amusing us genially by tactful play on her genteel inadequacies as a religious; while the Manciple is hardly described at all, but made the occasion of a satire on lawyers.

The Knight, the Squire, the Yeoman, the Clerk of Oxford, Parish Priest, and Franklin he treats seriously, though with greater or less reverence or familiarity. The Summoner and the Pardoner are drawn with uncommon stridency. Chaucer's reticence is almost all gone, as if he felt the decks must be cleared to deal with so blatant an impostor as the latter: Chaucer is unusually aggressive. But there is no disgust, dismay, or cynicism in his portraits of either. They may be stronger and more rank than the other characters, but that makes Chaucer relish them the more. He enjoys them as he enjoys the Friar and the Monk.

The relish with which Chaucer describes the ordinary things of life is one of his fundamental characteristics. He revels in the fact that things are what they are, and it is the uniqueness of each object and experience which delights him. Thus, in the Canon's Yeoman's Prologue a man over-takes the pilgrims on a horse all flecked with foam from hard riding and he himself dripping with sweat, and Chaucer, relishing this sight of a forehead oozing liquid like a still, cries,

> But it was joye for to seen him swete!

A strange enthusiasm! Chaucer sees the Yeoman sweating as no other man ever sweated; and in the same spirit he writes of a *horsly* horse and a *manly* man, creatures fully themselves, brimming over with the characteristics of their kind. And this is why so many of the characters in the Prologue seem outstanding in some way: there is no Pardoner like this one (693); no one has a better cellar than the Franklin (342); no man has campaigned as often as the Knight (55). Five characters are called worthy (43, 269, 283, 360, 459), and this word probably means not only 'distinguished' or 'excellent,' but also 'having the appropriate qualities' (see Glossary). Two of Chaucer's favourite adverbs are *ful* and *wel*—for example, "ful simple and coy" (119), "a ful solempne man" (209), "weel purtreye and write" (96), "Wel loved he by the morwe a sope in win" (334). By these simple words Chaucer thickens the soup. He was never one for mere water.

He often describes with unashamed enjoyment characteristics which in a less creative mood he would doubtless admit to be immoral, and condemn. And it is important to appreciate that if Chaucer plays the reforming preacher in the Prologue at all it is in the characters he treats seriously, and he does so by demonstrating in them the ideal. On the other hand much of Chaucer's comedy depends on an appeal to our sense of what his characters ought to be, to our sense of their incongruity. But they are not intended to reform anything. Chaucer's comedy is not corrective, his laughter is not surgical. He accepts the incongruity of sin or hypocrisy or crime and uses it to make us laugh.

Accordingly no personal malice or feeling of insecurity, no just indignation or moral horror, seeps through these lines about the Friar:

> He knew the tavernes wel in al the toun, . . . (240-251.)

The wit of these lines, their irony, and the play on such words as *honest* (246) and *profit* (249), are ends in themselves. In them Chaucer shows how he enjoys this hypocrite.[1]

And when Chaucer with innocent incongruity sandwiches the Franklin's dagger between mention of his being a magistrate and a sheriff, it is just possible that he is again evincing this serene view of life, in an acceptance of its multifarious variety as one great and subtle comedy.[2]

Pilgrimages

The occasion of the *Canterbury Tales* is a pilgrimage from Southwark to Canterbury. The purpose of such a pilgrimage was to venerate a shrine, to do penance for sin, to be healed of some sickness, or to give thanks (*cf.* l. 18, and ll. 77-78). Of shrines abroad the favourites were that of St James the Greater at Compostella in Galicia (N.W. Spain), that of St Peter and many more saints in Rome, that of the Magi at Cologne, and the holy places in Jerusalem. The Wife of Bath has been to all these (463-466). In England favourites were the shrine of the Blessed Virgin at Walsingham in Norfolk, and of St Thomas[3] at

---

[1] See also THE MERCHANT and SUMMONER for similar discussion.

[2] But remember the last paragraphs of "Chaucer's Work" (p. 13) and "The Canterbury Tales" (p. 19).

[3] Thomas à Becket was Archbishop of Canterbury when murdered in his own church by knights of King Henry II on December 29, 1170, and he was canonized in 1173.

Canterbury. And it is to his shrine that Chaucer's pilgrims are going (16–18). On arriving at the Cathedral they would find the tomb splendidly decorated with the offerings made there of gold and jewels, for the church granted special spiritual benefits to those who piously made the pilgrimage.

The pilgrims are travelling in a crowd partly for protection from the hazards of medieval travel, especially robbers such as attacked Chaucer himself in 1390 when he was carrying some £20 of the king's money as Clerk of the Works. Some medieval roads seemed as thickly covered with pilgrims as the heavens with stars, so that in Spain the Milky Way was called "the Santiago Road" (the road to St James), and in England "the Walsingham Way."

A pilgrimage was frequently a sort of bank-holiday excursion as well, sometimes to the exclusion of all religion. This we suspect of the pilgrimages made by the Wife of Bath (463–467), whose extensive travels indicate her love of holiday, not her devotion. The Miller leads Chaucer's pilgrims with his bagpipe (565–566), and the tales themselves are the entertainment that makes a hard journey easier. In Chaucer's day the reforming sect called the Lollards objected to pilgrimages partly because of their irreligious features; and it is true that they were particularly attractive to the idler and the swindler because special charity was given to all apparent pilgrims.

It is in response to the disturbing call of spring—"So priketh hem nature in hir corages"—that Chaucer's folk long to go on a pilgrimage, though devotion may be their end. They have a pious reason for what is nevertheless an outing over the hills and far away. They feel romance as well as religion. We have, in fact, that same mixture of motives that we find in the Tales—"*sentence*" and "*solas*"

(798). Chaucer is the first in literature to convey this mixture of sentiments by beginning a poem about a pilgrimage with the description of spring which conventionally began a medieval romantic poem.

A Note on the Text

The text is based on the manuscript formerly belonging to Lord Ellesmere, and now in the Henry E. Huntington Library, San Marino, California. Departures from this MS. (which is referred to as *El*) are recorded in the footnotes, along with a selection of variant readings from other manuscripts, in particular:

Hg=Hengwrt MS. 154, now in the National Library of Wales, Aberystwyth.

Gg=Cambridge University Library MS. Gg.4.27.

Cp=Corpus Christi College, Oxford MS. 188.

El and *Hg* were probably written in the first decade of the fifteenth century, *Cp* in the second, and *Gg* in the third or fourth.

All readings are taken from the Chaucer Society's print of these MSS., corrected in respect of the Ellesmere text from the facsimile edition of that manuscript and from collations published by E. Flugel and D. Everett.

The following changes have been made in the spelling found in the MSS.:

i, ai, ei, oi are regularly printed instead of *y, ay, ey, oy* (and *vice versa*) when this procedure helps the modern reader to identify the form: *e.g., knight, veine* for MS. *knyght, veyne.*

As regards *c* and *k, i* and *j, u* and *v*, the text conforms as far as possible to modern usage.

Final *-t3* is printed as *ts* (*e.g., servants* for *seruant3*).

The variant forms of the final *-r(e)* in *hir(e)* are all represented by *-r*.

THE PROLOGUE TO
THE CANTERBURY TALES

WHAN that Aprill[1] with hise shoures soote
The droghte of March hath perced to the roote,
And bathed every veine in swich licour,
Of which vertu engendred is the flour;
Whan Zephirus eek with his sweete breeth
Inspired hath in every holt and heeth
The tendre croppes; and the yonge sonne
Hath in the Ram his half[2] cours yronne;
And smale foweles maken melodye,
That slepen al the night with open eye,   10
So priketh hem nature in hir corages:
Thanne longen folk to goon on pilgrimages,
And palmeres for to seken straunge strondes,
To ferne halwes cowthe in sondry londes.
And specially fram every shires ende
Of Engelond, to Caunterbury they wende,
The hooly blisful martyr for to seke,
That hem hath holpen whan that they were seeke.

Bifil that in that seson on a day
In Southwerk at the Tabard as I lay,   20
Redy to wenden on my pilgrimage
To Caunterbury with ful devout corage,

[1] *Hg*, Aueryll.
[2] *Some MSS.*, halfe.

At night were come into that hostelrye
Wel nine and twenty in a compaignye
Of sondry folk, by aventure yfalle
In felaweshipe, and pilgrimes were they alle
That toward Caunterbury wolden ride.
The chambres and the stables weren wide,
And wel we weren esed atte beste.
And shortly, whan the sonne was to reste,   30
So hadde I spoken with hem everichon
That I was of hir felaweshipe anon,
And made forward erly for to rise,
To take oure wey theras I yow devise.
But nathelees, whil I have time and space,
Er that I ferther in this tale pace,
Me thinketh it acordaunt to resoun
To telle yow al the condicioun
Of ech of hem, so as it semed me,
And whiche they were, and of what degree,   40
And eek in what array that they were inne:
And at a knight than wol I first biginne.

A KNIGHT ther was, and that a worthy man,
That fro the time that he first bigan
To riden out, he loved chivalrye,
Trouthe and honour, fredom and curteisye.
Ful worthy was he in his lordes werre,
And therto hadde he riden, no man ferre,
As wel in cristendom as in hethenesse,
And evere honoured for his worthynesse.   50
At Alisaundre he was, whan it was wonne.
Ful ofte time he hadde the bord bigonne

Aboven alle nacions in Pruce.
In Lettow hadde he reised and in Ruce,
No cristen man so ofte of his degree.
In Gernade at the seege eek hadde he be
Of Algezir, and ridden in Belmarye.
At Lieis was he, and at Satalye,
Whan they were wonne; and in the Grete See
At many a noble armee hadde he be.   60
At mortal batailles hadde he been fiftene,
And foughten for oure feith at Tramissene
In listes thries, and ay slain his foo.
This ilke worthy knight hadde been also
Somtime with the lord of Palatye
Again another hethen in Turkye,
And everemoore he hadde a soverein pris.
And though that he were worthy, he was wis,
And of his port as meeke as is a maide:
He nevere yet no vileinye ne saide   70
In al his lif unto no maner wight.
He was a verray parfit gentil knight.
But for to tellen yow of his array:
His hors weren goode, but he was nat gay;
Of fustian he wered a gypoun
Al bismotered with his habergeoun,
For he was late ycome from his viage,
And wente for to doon his pilgrimage.

    With him ther was his sone, a yong SQUIER,
A lovyere and a lusty bacheler,   80
With lockes crulle as they were leid in presse.
Of twenty yeer of age he was, I gesse.

Of his stature he was of evene lengthe,
And wonderly delivere and of greet strengthe.
And he hadde been somtime in chivachye
In Flaundres, in Artois and Picardye,
And born him weel, as of so litel space,
In hope to stonden in his lady grace.
Embrouded was he, as it were a meede,
Al ful of fresshe floures white and reede.   90
Singinge he was, or floytinge, al the day:
He was as fressh as is the monthe of May.
Short was his gowne with sleves longe and wide.
Wel coude he sitte on hors and faire ride;
He coude songes make and wel endite,
Juste and eek daunce, and weel purtreye and write.
So hoote he lovede that by nightertale
He slepte namoore than dooth a nightingale.
Curteis he was, lowely, and servisable,
And carf biforn his fader at the table.   100

    A YEMAN hadde he and servants namo
At that time, for him liste ride so.
And he was clad in cote and hood of grene.
A sheef of pecok arwes, bright and kene,
Under his belt he bar ful thriftily;
Wel coude he dresse his takel yemanly—
Hise arwes drouped noght with fetheres lowe—
And in his hand he baar a mighty bowe.
A not-heed hadde he, with a broun visage.
Of wodecraft wel coude he al the usage.   110
Upon his arm he baar a gay bracer,
And by his side a swerd and a bokeler,

And on that oother side a gay daggere
Harneised wel and sharpe as point of spere.
A Cristophere on his brest of silver sheene;
An horn he bar, the bawdric was of grene.
A forster was he, soothly, as I gesse.

Ther was also a nonne, A PRIORESSE,
That of hir smiling was ful simple and coy.
Hir gretteste ooth was but by Seint Loy,   120
And she was cleped Madame Eglentine.
Ful weel she soong the service divine,
Entuned in hir nose ful semely,[1]
And Frenssh she spak ful faire and fetisly
After the scole of Stratford atte Bowe,
For Frenssh of Paris was to hir unknowe.
At mete wel ytaught was she withalle:
She leet no morsel from hir lippes falle,
Ne wette hir fingres in hir sauce depe;
Wel coude she carie a morsel, and wel kepe   130
That no drope ne fille upon hir brist.
In curteisye was set ful muchel hir list:
Hir over lippe wiped she so clene
That in hir coppe ther was no ferthing sene
Of grece, whan she dronken hadde hir draughte;
Ful semely after hir mete she raughte.
And sikerly she was of greet desport,
And ful plesaunt and amiable of port,
And peined hir to countrefete cheere
Of court, and to[2] been estatlich of manere,   140

---

[1] *El*, semeely.
[2] *Hg omits* to.

And to ben holden digne of reverence.
But, for to speken of hir conscience,
She was so charitable and so pitous
She wolde wepe if that she saugh a mous
Caught in a trappe, if it were deed or bledde.
Of smale houndes hadde she that she fedde
With rosted flessh, or milk and wastel breed;
But soore wepte she if any[1] of hem were deed,
Or if men smoot it with a yerde smerte,
And al was conscience and tendre herte.   150
Ful semily hir wimpul pinched was,
Hir nose tretis, hir eyen greye as glas,
Hir mouth ful smal and therto softe and reed.
But sikerly she hadde a fair forheed—
It was almoost a spanne brood, I trowe,
For, hardily, she was nat undergrowe.
Ful fetis was hir cloke, as I was war.
Of smal coral aboute hir arm she bar
A peire of bedes, gauded al with grene,
And theron heng a brooch of gold ful sheene, 160
On which ther[2] was first write a crowned A,
And after, *Amor vincit omnia.*

Another nonne with hir hadde she,
That was hir chapeleyne, and preestes thre.

A MONK ther was, a fair for the maistrye,
An outridere that lovede venerye,
A manly man, to been an abbot able.

---

[1] any: *other MSS.*, (o)on(e).
[2] *Some MSS. omit* ther, *Gg omits* first.

Ful many a deintee hors hadde he in stable,
And, whan he rood, men mighte his bridel
     heere
Ginglen in a whistlinge wind als cleere,   170
And eek as loude, as dooth the chapel belle,
Theras this lord was kepere of the celle.
The reule of Seint Maure or of Seint Beneit,
Bycause that it was old and somdel streit,
This ilke monk leet olde thinges pace
And heeld after the newe world the space.
He yaf nat of that text a pulled hen
That seith that hunters beth nat hooly men,
Ne that a monk whan he is recchelees
Is likned til a fissh that is waterlees—   180
This is to seyn, a monk out of his cloistre:
But thilke text heeld he nat worth an oystre—
And I seide his opinioun was good.
What sholde he studye, and make himselven wood
Upon a book in cloistre alwey to poure,
Or swinken with his handes, and laboure,
As Austin bit? How shal the world be served?
Lat Austin have his swink[1] to him reserved!
Therfore he was a prikasour aright.
Grehoundes he hadde as swift as fowel in
     flight;   190
Of priking and of hunting for the hare
Was al his lust, for no cost wolde he spare.
I seigh his sleves ypurfiled at the hond
With gris, and that the fineste of a lond;
And for to festne his hood under his chin

[1]*El*, his owene swink.

He hadde, of gold ywroght,[1] a ful curious pin.
A love knotte in the gretter ende ther was.
His heed was balled, that shoon as any glas,
And eek his face, as it hadde been enoint.
He was a lord ful fat and in good point;   200
His eyen stepe and rollinge in his heed,
That stemed as a forneis of a leed;
His bootes souple, his hors in greet estaat.
Now certeinly he was a fair prelaat.
He nas nat pale as a forpined goost.
A fat swan loved he best of any roost.
His palfrey was as broun as is a berye.

A FRERE ther was, a wantowne and a merye,
A limitour, a ful solempne man.
In alle the ordres foure is noon that can   210
So muchel of daliaunce and fair langage.
He hadde maad ful many a mariage
Of yonge wommen at his owene cost.
Unto his ordre he was a noble post.
And wel biloved and famulier was he
With frankeleins overal in his contree,
And with[2] worthy wommen of the toun:
For he hadde power of confessioun,
As seide himself, moore than a curat,
For of his ordre he was licenciat.   220
Ful swetely herde he confessioun,
And plesaunt was his absolucioun.
He was an esy man to yeve penaunce

---

[1] *Some MSS.*, wroght.
[2] *Hg.* And eek with.

Theras he wiste to have a good pitaunce;
For unto a poure ordre for to yive
Is signe that a man is wel yshrive;
For if he yaf, he dorste make avaunt,
He wiste that a man was repentaunt.
For many a man so hard is of his herte
He may nat wepe althogh him soore smerte.　　230
Therfore instede of wepinge and preyeres
Men moote yeve silver to the poure fr
His tipet was ay farsed ful of knives
And pinnes, for to yeven yonge[1] wives.
And certeinly he hadde a murye note,
Wel coude he singe and pleyen on a rote.
Of yeddinges he baar outrely the pris.
His necke whit was as the flour de lis.
Therto he strong was as a champioun.
He knew the tavernes wel in al the toun,　　240
And everich hostiler and tappestere
Bet than a lazar or a beggestere.
For unto swich a worthy man as he
Acorded nat, as by his facultee,
To have with sike lazars aqueintaunce.
It is nat honeste, it may nat avaunce,
For to deelen with no swich poraille,
But al with riche, and selleres of vitaille.
And overal theras profit sholde arise
Curteis he was and lowely of servise;　　250
Ther nas no man nowher so vertuous.
He was the beste beggere in his hous,
[And yaf a certein ferme for the graunt　　252 b

___
[1] yonge: *some MSS.*, faire.

Noon of his bretheren cam ther in his haunt.252 c[1]]
For thogh a widwe hadde noght a sho,
So plesaunt was his *In principio*,
Yet wolde he have a ferthing er he wente.
His purchas was wel bettre than his rente.
And rage he coude as it were right a whelpe
In lovedayes, ther[2] coude he muchel helpe.
For ther he was nat lik a cloistrer[3]
With a thredbare cope, as is a poure scoler,   260
But he was lik a maister or a pope.
Of double worstede was his semicope,
That rounded as a belle out of the presse.
Somwhat he lipsed for his wantownesse,
To make his Englissh sweete upon his tonge.
And in his harping, whan that he hadde songe,
Hise eyen twinkled in his heed aright
As doon the sterres in the frosty night.
This worthy limitour was cleped Huberd.

A MARCHANT was ther with a forked berd,   270
In motlee[4] and hye on horse he sat,
Upon his heed a Flaundrissh bevere hat,
His bootes clasped faire and fetisly.
Hise resons he spak ful solempnely,
Sowninge alwey th'encrees of his winning.
He wolde the see were kept for any thing
Bitwixe Middelburgh and Orewelle.
Wel coude he in eschaunge sheeldes selle.
This worthy man ful wel his wit bisette:

---

[1] *In Hg and a few other MSS. only.*
[2] *Hg omits* ther.
[3] *Gg*, cloysterer.
[4] *Some MSS.*, motteley(e).

Ther wiste no wight that he was in dette,　　280
So estatly was he of his governaunce,
With his bargaines and with his chevissaunce.
For sothe he was a worthy man withalle,
But sooth to seyn, I noot how men him calle.

　A CLERK ther was of Oxenford also,
That unto logic hadde longe ygo,
And[1] leene was his hors as is a rake.
And he nas nat right fat, I undertake,
But looked holwe, and therto sobrely.
Ful thredbare was his overeste courtepy,　　290
For he hadde geten him yet no benefice,
Ne was so worldly for to have office.
For him was levere have at his beddes heed
Twenty bookes, clad in blak or reed,
Of Aristotle and his philosophye,
Than robes riche or fithele or gay sautrye.
But al be that he was a philosophre
Yet hadde he but litel gold in cofre:
But al that he mighte of his freendes hente
On bookes and on lerninge he it spente,　　300
And bisily gan for the soules preye
Of hem that yaf him wherwith to scoleye.
Of studye took he moost cure and moost heede.
Noght o word spak he moore than was neede,
And that was seid in forme and reverence,
And short and quik and ful of hy sentence.
Sowninge in moral vertu was his speche,
And gladly wolde he lerne, and gladly teche.

[1] And: *some MSS.*, As.

A SERGEANT OF THE LAWE, war and wis,
That often hadde been at the Parvis,   310
Ther was also, ful riche of excellence.
Discreet he was, and of greet reverence:
He semed swich, hise wordes weren so wise.
Justice he was ful often in assise
By patente and by plein commissioun.
For his science and for his heigh renoun
Of fees and robes hadde he many oon.
So greet a purchasour was nowher noon.
Al was fee simple to him, in effect;
His purchasing mighte nat been infect.   320
Nowher so bisy a man as he ther nas,
And yet he semed bisier than he was.
In termes hadde he caas and doomes alle
That from the time of King William were falle.
Therto he coude endite and make a thing:
Ther coude no wight pinchen at his writing.
And every statut coude he plein by rote.
He rood but hoomly in a medlee cote,
Girt with a ceint of silk with barres smale.
Of his array telle I no lenger tale.   330

A FRANKELEIN was in his compaignye:
Whit was his heed[1] as is a daiesye.
Of his complexioun he was sangwin.
Wel loved he by the morwe a sope in win.
To liven in delit was evere his wone,
For he was Epicurus owene sone,
That heeld opinioun that plein delit.

---

[1] heed: *other MSS.*, berd.

Was verray felicitee parfit.
An housholdere, and that a greet, was he,
Seint Julian was he in his contree.   340
His breed, his ale, was alweys after oon,
A bettre envined man was nevere noon;
Withoute bake mete was nevere his hous,
Of fissh and flessh, and that so plenteuous,
It snewed in his hous of mete and drinke,
Of alle deintees that men coude thinke.
After the sondry sesons of the yeer
So chaunged he his mete and his soper.
Ful many a fat partrich hadde he in muwe,
And many a breem and many a luce in stuwe.   350
Wo was his cook but if his sauce were
Poynaunt and sharpe, and redy al his geere.
His table dormant in his halle alway
Stood redy covered al the longe day.
At sessiouns ther was he lord and sire
Ful ofte time he was knight of the shire.
An anlaas and a gipser al of silk
Heeng at his girdel, whit as morne milk.
A shirreve hadde he been and countour;[1]
Was nowher swich a worthy vavasour.   360

AN HABERDASSHERE and A CARPENTER,
A WEBBE, A DYERE and A TAPICER,
And they were clothed alle in o liveree
Of a solempne and a greet fraternitee.
Ful fressh and newe hir geere apiked was.
Hir knives were chaped noght with bras

[1] *Some MSS.*, and a countour.

But al with silver, wroght ful clene and weel,
Hir girdles and hir pouches everydeel.
Wel semed ech of hem a fair burgeis
To sitten in a yeldehalle on a deis: 370
Everich for the wisdom that he can
Was shaply for to been an alderman,
For catel hadde they ynogh, and rente,
And eek hir wives wolde it wel assente.
And elles certein were they to blame!
It is ful fair to been ycleped 'madame,'
And goon to vigilies al bifore,
And have a mantel royalliche ybore.

    A COOK they hadde with hem for the nones
To boille the chiknes with the marybones,   380
And poudre marchant tart, and galingale.
Wel coude he knowe a draughte of Londoun ale.
He coude rooste and sethe and boille[1] and frye,
Maken mortreux and wel bake a pie.
But greet harm was it, as it thoughte me,
That on his shine a mormal hadde he.
For blankmanger, that made he with the beste.

    A SHIPMAN was ther, woninge fer by weste:
For aught I woot he was of Dertemouthe.
He rood upon a rouncy, as he couthe,   390
In a gowne of falding to the knee.
A daggere hanginge on a laas hadde he
About his nekke, under his arm adoun.
The hoote somer hadde maad his hewe al broun.

---

[1] *Hg*, broille.

And certeinly he was a good felawe.
Ful many a draughte of win had he drawe[1]
Fro Burdeuxward whil that the chapman sleepe.
Of nice conscience took he no keepe.
If that he faught and hadde the hier hond,
By water he sente hem hoom to every lond.   400
But of his craft, to rekene wel his tides,
His stremes and his daungers him bisides,
His herberwe and his moone, his lodemenage,
Ther nas noon swich from Hull to Cartage.
Hardy he was, and wis to undertake.
With many a tempest hadde his berd been shake.
He knew alle the havenes as they were
Fro Gootlond to the Cape of Finistere,
And every cryke in Britaigne and in Spaine.
His barge ycleped was the Maudelaine.   410

With us ther was A DOCTOUR OF PHYSIC,
In al this world ne was ther noon him lik
To speke of physic and of surgerye,
For he was grounded in astronomye.
He kepte his pacient a ful greet deel
In houres by his magic natureel;
Wel coude he fortunen the ascendent
Of hise images for his pacient;
He knew the cause of everich maladye,
Were it of hoot or coold or moiste or drye,   420
And where they engendred, and of what humour.
He was a verray parfit practisour.
The cause yknowe, and of his harm the roote,

---

[1] *Gg*, Idrawe.

Anon he yaf the sike man his boote.
Ful redy hadde he hise apothecaries
To sende him drogges and his letuaries.
For ech of hem made oother for to winne,
Hir frendshipe nas nat newe to biginne.
Wel knew he the olde Esculapius,
And Deiscorides, and eek Rufus,[1]   430
Olde Ypocras, Haly and Galyen;
Serapion, Razis and Avicen;
Averrois, Damascien and Constantin;
Bernard and Gatesden and Gilbertin.
Of his diete mesurable was he,
For it was of no superfluitee,
But of greet norissing and digestible.
His studye was but litel on the Bible.
In sangwin and in pers he clad was al,
Lined with taffata and with sendal: 440
And yet he was but esy of dispence;
He kepte that he wan in pestilence.
For gold in physic is a cordial,
Therfore he lovede gold in special.

    A GOOD WIF was ther of biside Bathe,
But she was somdel deef and that was scathe.
Of clooth-making she hadde swich an haunt
She passed hem of Ypres and of Gaunt.
In al the parisshe wif ne was ther noon
That to the offringe bifore hir sholde goon.   450
And if ther dide, certein, so wrooth was she
That she was out of alle charitee.

    [1] *So most MSS., but Hg,* Rusus, *El,* Risus.

Hir coverchiefs ful fine weren of ground:
I dorste swere they weyeden ten pound
That on a Sonday weren upon hir heed.
Hir hosen weren of fin scarlet reed,
Ful streite yteyd, and shoes ful moiste and newe.
Boold was hir face, and fair, and reed of hewe.
She was a worthy womman al hir live;
Housbondes at chirche dore she hadde five,   460
Withouten oother compaignye in youthe—
But therof nedeth nat to speke as nowthe.
And thries hadde she been at Jerusalem.
She hadde passed many a straunge strem;
At Rome she hadde been, and at Boloigne,
In Galice at Seint Jame, and at Cologne;
She coude muchel of wandringe by the weye.
Gat-tothed was she, soothly for to seye.
Upon an amblere esily she sat,
Ywimpled wel, and on hir heed an hat   470
As brood as is a bokeler or a targe;
A foot-mantel aboute hir hipes large,
And on hir feet a paire of spores sharpe.
In felaweshipe wel coude she laughe and carpe.
Of remedies of love she knew perchaunce,
For she coude of that art the olde daunce.

A good man was ther of religioun,
And was A POURE PERSOUN of a toun;
But riche he was of hooly thoght and werk.
He was also a lerned man, a clerk   480
That Cristes gospel trewely wolde preche;
His parisshens devoutly wolde he teche.

Benigne he was, and wonder diligent,
And in adversitee ful pacient,
And swich he was preved ofte sithes.
Ful looth were him to cursen for hise tithes,
But rather wolde he yeven, out of doute,
Unto his poure parisshens aboute
Of his offring and eek of his substaunce;
He coude in litel thing have suffisaunce.   490
Wid was his parisshe, and houses fer asonder,
But he ne lefte nat, for rein ne thonder,
In siknesse nor in meschief to visite
The ferreste in his parisshe, muche and lite,
Upon his feet, and in his hand a staf.
This noble ensample to his sheepe he yaf,
That firste he wroghte, and afterward[1] he
          taughte.
Out of the gospel he tho wordes caughte,
And this figure he added eek therto,
That if gold ruste, what shal iren do?   500
For if a preest be foul, on whom we truste,
No wonder is a lewed man to ruste!
And shame it is, if a prest take keepe,
A shiten shepherde and a clene sheepe.
Wel oghte a preest ensample for to yeve
By his clennesse how that his sheepe sholde live.
He sette nat his benefice to hire,
And leet his sheepe encombred in the mire,
And ran to Londoun, unto Seint Poules,
To seken him a chauntrye for soules,   510
Or with a bretherhed to been withholde;

---

[1] *El* afterward that he.

But dwelleth at hoom and kepeth[1] wel his folde
So that the wolf ne made it nat miscarye.
He was a shepherde and noght a mercenarye.
And though he hooly were, and vertuous,
He was nat to sinful men despitous,
Ne of his speche daungerous ne digne,
But in his teching discreet and benigne.
To drawen folk to hevene by fairnesse
By good ensample, this was his bisynesse.   520
But it were any persone obstinat,
Whatso he were, of heigh or lough estat,
Him wolde he snibben sharply for the nonis.
A bettre preest I trowe that nowher noon is.
He waiteth[2] after no pompe and reverence,
Ne maked him a spiced conscience.
But Cristes loore and Hise Apostles twelve
He taughte, but first he folwed it himselve.

With him ther was A PLOWMAN was his
    brother,
That hadde ylad of dong ful many a fother.   530
A trewe swinkere and a good was he,
Livinge in pees and parfit charitee.
God loved he best with al his hoole herte
At alle times, thogh he[3] gamed or smerte,
And thanne his neighebore right as himselve.
He wolde thresshe, and therto dyke and delve,
For Cristes sake, for every poure wight,

---

[1] *Hg and some MSS.*, dwelte . . . kepte.
[2] *Hg, Gg,* waited.
[3] *Hg, Gg, Cp,* hym.

Withouten hire, if it lay in his might.
Hise tithes payde he ful faire and wel,
Bothe of his propre swink and his catel.   540
In a tabard he rood upon a mere.

    Ther was also a Reve and a Millere,
A Somnour and a Pardoner also,
A Maunciple and myself—ther were namo.

    THE MILLERE was a stout carl for the nones,
Ful big he was of brawn and eek of bones;
That proved wel, for overal ther he cam,
At wrastlinge he wolde have alwey the ram.
He was short-sholdred, brood, a thicke knarre;
Ther was no dore that he nolde heve of harre, 550
Or breke it at a renning with his heed.
His berd as any sowe or fox was reed,
And therto brood as though it were a spade.
Upon the cope right of his nose he hade
A werte, and theron stood a toft of heris,
Reed as the brustles of a sowes eris.
Hise nosethirles blake were and wide.
A swerd and bokeler bar he by his side.
His mouth as greet was as a greet forneis.
He was a janglere and a goliardeis,   560
And that was moost of sinne and harlotries.
Wel coude he stelen corn and tollen thries—
And yet he hadde a thombe of gold, pardee.
A whit cote and a blew hood wered he.
A baggepipe wel coude he blowe and sowne,
And therwithal he broghte us out of towne.

A gentil MAUNCIPLE was ther of a temple,
Of which achatours mighte take exemple
For to be wise in byinge of vitaille:
For wheither that he payde or took by taille,   570
Algate he waited so in his achaat
That he was ay biforn and in good staat.
Now is nat that of God a ful fair grace,
That swich a lewed mannes wit shal pace
The wisdom of an heepe of lerned men?
Of maistres hadde he mo than thries ten
That weren of lawe expert and curious;
Of whiche ther weren a duszeine in that hous
Worthy to been stiwardes of rente and lond
Of any lord that is in Engelond,   580
To maken him live by his propre good
In honour, dettelees, but if he were wood,
Or live as scarsly as him list desire
And able for to helpen al a shire
In any caas that mighte falle or happe.
And yet this manciple sette hir aller cappe.

THE REVE was a sclendre coleric man;
His berd was shave as ny as ever he can;
His heer was by his eris ful round yshorn;
His tope was docked lik a preest biforn;   590
Ful longe were his legges and ful lene,
Ylik a staf, ther was no calf ysene.
Wel coude he kepe a gerner and a binne:
Ther was noon auditour coude of him winne.
Wel wiste he by the droghte and by the rein
The yeldinge of his seed and of his grein.

His lordes sheepe, his neet, his daierye
His swin, his hors, his stoor, and his pultrye
Was hoolly in this reves governing,
And by his covenant yaf the rekening   600
Sin that his lord was twenty yeer of age.
Ther coude no man bringe him in arrerage:
Ther nas baillif, ne hierde, nor oother hine,
That he knew[1] his sleighte and his covine.
They were adrad of him as of the deeth.
His woning was ful faire upon an heeth;
With grene trees shadwed was his place.
He coude bettre than his lord purchace:
Ful riche he was astored prively.
His lord wel coude he plesen subtilly   610
To yeve and lene him of his owene good,
And have a thank, and yet a gowne and hood.
In youthe he hadde lerned a good myster:
He was a wel good wrighte, a carpenter.
This reve sat upon a ful good stot
That was al pomely grey, and highte Scot.
A long surcote of pers upon he hade,
And by his side he baar a rusty blade.
Of Northfolk was this reve of which I telle,
Biside a toun men clepen Baldeswelle.   620
Tucked he was as is a frere aboute,
And evere he rood the hindreste of oure route.

A SOMONOUR was ther with us in that place,
That hadde a fir-reed cherubinnes face,
For saucefleem he was, with eyen narwe.

---

[1] *Hg and some other MSS.*, he ne knew.

As hoot he was, and lecherous, as a sparwe,
With scaled browes blake and piled berd.
Of his visage children were aferd.
Ther nas quik-silver, litarge, ne brimstoon,
Boras, ceruce, ne oille of tartre noon,   630
Ne oinement that wolde clense and bite,
That him mighte helpen of the whelkes white,
Nor of the knobbes sittinge on his chekes.
Wel loved he garleek, oinons, and eek lekes,
And for to drinken strong win, reed as blood.
Thanne wolde he speke and crye as he were wood.
And whan that he wel dronken hadde the win,
Thanne wolde he speke no word but Latin.[1]
A fewe termes hadde he, two or thre,
That he had lerned out of som decree: 640
No wonder is, he herde it al the day.
And eek ye knowen wel how that a jay
Can clepen, "Watte," as wel as can the Pope.
But whoso coude in oother thing him grope
Thanne hadde he spent al his philosophye.
Ay, "*Questio quid iuris*," wolde he crye.
He was a gentil harlot and a kinde;
A bettre felawe sholde men noght finde:
He wolde suffre for a quart of win
A good felawe to have his concubin   650
A twelf-monthe, and excuse him atte fulle.
Ful prively a finch eek coude he pulle.
And if he foond owher a good felawe,
He wolde techen him to have noon awe,
In swich caas, of the ercedekenes curs,

[1] *ll.* 637-638 *omitted Hg.*

But if a mannes soule were in his purs:
For in his purs he sholde ypunisshed be.
"Purs is the ercedekenes helle!" seide he.
But wel I woot he lied right indede—
Of cursing oghte ech gilty man him[1] drede,   660
For curs wol slee right as assoilling savith,
And also war him of a *Significavit*.
In daunger hadde he at his owene gise
The yonge girls of the diocise,
And knew hir conseil and was al hir reed.
A gerland hadde he set upon his heed
As greet as it were for an ale-stake.
A bokeleer hadde he maad him of a cake.

With him ther was[2] a gentil PARDONER
Of Rouncivale, his freend and his compeer,   670
That streight was comen fro the court of Rome.
Ful loude he soong, "Com hider, love, to me!"
This somonour bar to him a stif burdoun;
Was nevere trompe of half so greet a soun.
This pardoner hadde heer as yelow as wex,
But smothe it heeng as dooth a strike of flex;
By ounces henge hise lockes that he hadde,
And therwith he hise shuldres overspradde,
But thinne it lay, by colpons, oon and oon.
But hood, for jolitee, wered he noon,   680
For it was trussed up in his walet.
Him thoughte he rood al of the newe jet.
Dischevelee, save his cappe, he rood al bare.

---

[1] him: *some MSS.*, to; *El, Gg, Hg omit.*
[2] was: *Hg, Gg, and some MSS.*, rood.

Swiche glaringe eyen hadde he as an hare.
A vernicle hadde he sowed upon his cappe.
His walet biforn[1] him in his lappe,
Bretful of pardoun comen from Rome al hoot.
A vois he hadde as smal as hath a goot;
No berd hadde he, ne nevere sholde have,
As smothe it was as it were late shave;   690
I trowe he were a gelding or a mare.
But of his craft, fro Berwik into Ware,
Ne was ther swich another pardoner.
For in his male he hadde a pilwe-beer,
Which that he seide was Oure Lady veil.
He seide he hadde a gobet of the seil
That Seint Peter hadde whan that he wente
Upon the see, til Jhesu Crist him hente.
He hadde a crois of latoun, ful of stones,
And in a glas he hadde pigges bones.   700
But with thise relices, whan that he fond
A poure persoun dwellinge up on lond,
Upon a day he gat him moore moneye
Than that the person gat in monthes tweye.
And thus, with feyned flaterye and japes,
He made the persoun and the peple his apes.
But trewely to tellen, atte laste,
He was in chirche a noble ecclesiaste:
Wel coude he rede a lessoun or a storye,
But alderbest he song an Offertorye,   710
For wel he wiste, whan that song was songe,
He moste preche, and wel affile his tonge
To winne silver as he ful wel coude;

---

[1] *Some MSS.*, walet lay biforn.

Therefore he song the murierly and loude.

Now have I toold you shortly in a clause
The staat, th'array, the nombre and eek the cause
Why that assembled was this compaignye
In Southwerk, at this gentil hostelrye,
That highte the Tabard, faste by the Belle.
But now is time to yow for to telle   720
How that we baren us that ilke night
Whan we were in that hostelrye alight,
And after wol I telle of oure viage,
And al the remenaunt of oure pilgrimage.
But first I pray yow, of youre curteisye,
That ye n'arette it nat my vileinye,
Thogh that I pleinly speke in this mateere
To telle yow hir wordes and hir cheere,
Ne thogh I speke hir wordes proprely.
For this ye knowen also wel as I,   730
Whoso shal telle a tale after a man,
He moot reherce, as ny as evere he can,
Everich a word, if it be in his charge,
Al speke he never so rudeliche or large,
Or ellis he moot telle his tale untrewe,
Or feyne thing, or finde wordes newe.
He may nat spare, althogh he were his brother.
He moot as wel seye o word as another.
Crist spak himself ful brode in hooly writ,
And wel ye woot no vileinye is it.   740
Eek Plato seith, whoso can him rede,
The wordes moote be cosin to the dede.
Also I prey yow to foryeve it me

Al have I nat set folk in hir degree,
Heere in this tale, as that they sholde stonde.
My wit is short, ye may wel understonde.

Greet chiere made oure hoost us everichon,
And to the soper sette he us anon;
He served us with vitaille at the beste.
Strong was the win and wel to drinke us leste. 750

A semely man OURE HOOST was withalle
For to been a marchal in an halle.
A large man he was with eyen stepe,
A fairer burgeis was ther noon in Chepe;
Boold of his speche, and wis, and well ytaught,
And of manhood him lacked[1] right naught.
Eek therto he was right a mirye man;
And after soper pleyen he bigan,
And spak of mirthe, amonges othere thinges,
Whan that we hadde maad oure rekeninges,   760
And seide thus: "Now, lordinges, trewely
Ye been to me right welcome hertely!
For by my trouthe, if that I shal nat lie,
I saugh nat this yeer so mirye a compaignye
At ones in this herberwe as is now—
Fain wolde I doon yow mirthe, wiste I how.
And of a mirthe I am right now bithoght
To doon yow ese—and it shal coste noght.

Ye goon to Caunterbury—God yow speede!
The blisful martyr quite yow youre meede!   770

[1] *Gg*, lakkede.

And wel I woot, as ye goon by the weye,
Ye shapen yow to talen and to pleye:
For, trewely, confort ne mirthe is noon
To ride by the weye doumb as the stoon.
And therfore wol I maken yow disport,
As I seide erst, and doon yow som confort.
And if yow liketh alle by oon assent
For to stonden at my juggement,
And for to werken as I shal yow seye,
Tomorwe, whan ye riden by the weye,   780
Now, by my fader soule, that is deed,
But if[1] ye be mirye I wol yeve yow min heed.
Hoold up youre hond withouten moore spechel"

Oure conseil was nat longe for to seche—
Us thoughte it was noght worth to make it wis,
And graunted him withouten moore avis,
And bad him seye his voirdit as him leste.

"Lordinges," quod he, "now herkneth for the
    beste,
But taak it nought, I prey yow, in desdein.
This is the point, to speken short and plein,   790
That ech of yow to shorte with oure weye,
In this viage shal telle tales tweye—
To Caunterburyward, I mene it so,
And homward he shal tellen othere two—
Of aventures that whilom han bifalle.
And which of yow that bereth him best of alle,
That is to seyn, that telleth in this caas

[1] *Hg and some other MSS., omit* if.

Tales of best sentence and moost solaas,
Shal have a soper at oure aller cost,
Heere in this place, sittinge by this post,　　800
Whan that we come again fro Caunterbury.
And for to make yow the moore mury,
I wol myself goodly with yow ride
Right at min owene cost, and be youre gide.
And whoso wole my juggement withseye
Shal paye al that we spenden by the weye.
And if ye vouchesauf that it be so,
Tel me anon, withouten wordes mo,
And I wol erly shape me therfore."

This thing was graunted and oure othes
　　　swore　　810
With ful glad herte, and preyden him also
That he wolde vouchesauf for to do so,
And that he wolde been oure governour,
And of our tales juge and reportour,
And sette a soper at a certein pris;
And we wol reuled been at his devis
In heigh and lough. And thus, by oon assent,
We been acorded to his juggement.
And therupon the win was fet anon.
We dronken, and to reste wente echon,　　820
Withouten any lenger taryinge.

Amorwe, whan that day gan for to springe,
Up roos oure hoost and was oure aller cok,
And gadrede us togidre alle in a flok,
And forth we riden, a litel moore than paas,

Unto the watering of Seint Thomas.
And there oure hoost bigan his hors areste,
And seide, "Lordinges, herkneth, if yow leste!
Ye woot youre foreward and it yow[1] recorde.
If evensong and morwesong accorde,   830
Lat se now who shal telle the firste tale.
As ever mote I drinke win or ale!
Whoso be rebel to my juggement
Shal paye for al that by the wey is spent.
Now draweth cut, er that we ferrer twinne;
He which that hath the shorteste shal biginne.
Sire Knight," quod he, "My maister and my lord,
Now draweth cut, for that is min accord.
Cometh neer!" quod he, "My lady Prioresse,
And ye, sire Clerk, lat be youre shame-
      fastnesse!   840
Ne studieth noght! Ley hond to, every man!"

    Anon to drawen every wight bigan.
And shortly, for to tellen as it was,
Were it by aventure, or sort, or cas,
The sothe is this: the cut fil to the knight,
Of which ful blithe and glad was every wight.
And[2] telle he moste his tale, as was resoun,
By foreward and by composicioun,
As ye han herd. What nedeth wordes mo?
An[3] whan this goode man saugh that it
      was so,   850

[1] it yow: *some MSS.*, ye it; *some (less authoritative) MSS.*, I it yow.
[2] And: *El*, A.
[3] An: *some MSS.*, And.

As he that wis was and obedient,
To kepe his foreward by his free assent,
He seide, "Sin I shal biginne the game,
What, welcome be the cut, a Goddes name!
Now lat us ride and herkneth what I seye!"

And with that word we riden forth oure weye;
And he bigan with right a mirye cheere
His tale anon, and seide in this manere:

NOTES

1–12. In this elaborate introduction with its balanced circum-locutions Chaucer uses common rhetorical devices and con-ventional epithets, yet gives an effect of novelty to details of the spring that can be paralleled either in earlier European poetry or in medieval encyclopædias. But nowhere better than in these mellifluous lines—the adjectives few and un-particular, the description so much taken for granted and free from strain—do we sense the delight with which men hailed the coming of spring when there were few of our modern comforts to mitigate the austerities of winter.

The meaning of ll. 1–4 is probably, 'When April with its genial showers has got right through the dryness of March, and soaked every vein of the earth (*or* of the plant) with that moisture, by the life-giving power of which the plant is born; when, also, the western wind ...'

1. *Aprill*. Probably pronounced with 'syllabic' *r* (Áperil).

7–8. The sun is 'young' because it is spring and it is just start-ing its annual journey about the earth (see Appendix III), having entered the sign of the Ram on March 12. The 'half course' is that half of the Ram through which it goes in April: for ll. 1–2 suggest that April is well under way, and in the Introduction to the Man of Law's Tale (B5) the date at that point in the pilgrimage—apparently an early point—is said to be the eighteenth of April.

9–11. Like the Squire (97–98) the birds feel the eager restless-ness of spring and consequently 'hardly sleep at all.'

12. *pilgrimages*. See Introduction, p. 33.

12–14. Though the syntax is not clear, the general meaning is. Probably in l. 13 *longen* should be understood after *pa meres*, and in l. 14 *to goon* before *to ferne*.

13. A palmer is described in *Piers Plowman*, A VI, 7. He carries

a staff, a bowl for eating, and a bag for storing food he has begged, and wears the signs of all the shrines he has visited— for example, the scallop-shell of St James at Compostella and the keys of Rome. The name probably derives from palm-leaves, the sign worn by the pilgrims returning from the Holy Places in Palestine.

17–18. Identical rhyme, the French *rime riche*. Unpleasant to the modern English ear, it was nevertheless cultivated in M.E. poetry, which was in many ways very 'French.' Chaucer sometimes used it even when the meaning and function of the rhyming words were the same.

20. There was an inn called the Tabard in Southwark in Chaucer's day.

33. 'we *made*.' The subject is implied by ll. 32 and 34 (*cf*. ll. 786 and 810–811).

43. THE KNIGHT. This portrait of a soldier is concerned chiefly with his extensive and brave campaigning (47–67), and with his virtues as a Christian knight (43–46 and 68–72). Four lines only are devoted to description of his appearance (73–76), and these, referring to his sober, work-a-day dress, serve really as a supplement to the picture of his virtues. No reference is made to an estate, nor to the duties a knight might be expected to perform in local government. (*Cf*. THE FRANKLIN.) He is presented as a model of the perfect military man described in the didactic literature of the later Middle Ages, but Chaucer specially emphasizes his career as a crusader, a Christian soldier fighting the infidel. Fighting had occurred at all the places he is said to have visited, and one man could have fought at them all; but otherwise there is nothing to suggest that Chaucer had a particular knight in mind.

His excellence is partly conveyed by stock words and phrases—*worthy* and *worthynesse* (five times), *honoured, he hadde a soverein pris*. But though these general terms chiefly concern his standing as a soldier, he is not rash and boorishly brave, but sensible and civilized (68–72). Fierce in the field, he is 'gentle' in the hall. This ideal is found in English as early as the O.E. poem, *Beowulf*.

Many knightly attributes are specified:

Chivalrye (45), see Glossary.

Trouthe (46) is 'loyalty.' He was 'true,' for example, to his lord (47 and 65) and to his fellow knights. Such personal relationships described in the literature of the Middle Ages were intense, and allegiance was maintained to the death. If the knight made a vow he did not break his 'troth.'

Fredom (46) is 'liberality,' or 'generosity.' It was also called *largesse*—a magnificent gesture of contempt for wealth (requiring much wealth to make it), another way of achieving glorious renown, and essentially a duty a 'gentle' man owed to his position and high-breeding. Something of the opposite is seen in the Merchant, so constantly absorbed in business, so constantly *respecting* money. But the virtue did not concern wealth alone: it was 'generosity' in every sphere, the renunciation, for example, of one's own rights for the sake of another grieved or offended by them, letting some one off a promise if to keep it pained them.

The Knight is graced with all the virtues and good manners to be found in one of good birth (72)—for etymologically that is what *gentle* means. The opposite of *gentleness* was *vileinye* (70), just as the opposite of the gentleman, the free man, was the villein, who, being in many respects a slave, working the land, making armour, building castles, had no wealth of his own with which to practise *fredom* or any other virtue of the 'free' man, and had no time to devote to winning honour. *Vileinye* was not, therefore, so much 'wickedness' as 'boorishness.' (*Cf.* THE PRIORESS, and ll. 726 and 740.)

On the other hand it was often argued that *gentleness* was determined by how you acted and not by how you were born. Gentle is as gentle does.

Curteisye (46) is 'good-breeding.' The young gentleman of the Middle Ages, such as the Squire, by serving as a lower officer in a great household, perhaps his father's, that of another gentleman, or of a great bishop or abbot, was taught an elaborate system of manners and of precedence. His instruction ranged from carving (99–100) to the discreet way of speaking to his superiors first thing in the morning! In some contexts, a 'courteous' man meant more particularly one whose manners were a delight to ladies, in others, rather one whose virtue it was to do to his neighbour as he would be done by. The Knight's courtesy is nearer the latter, and his Squire's the former. Meekness (69) and courtesy have for the Knight much in common.

Thus Chaucer interprets in a Christian way the ideals which in some medieval writers are purely those of a military class or of refined lovers. Thus the *honour* (46) loved by the Knight was not merely 'renown' but '*virtuous* renown' as a Christian soldier and gentleman. (*Cf.* THE PRIORESS.)

47–49. *his lordes werre* is either 'the war of Christ' (*i.e.*, the Crusades) or 'the king's war' (*i.e.*, the war between England and France). If the latter, it is the only reference to non-crusading warfare; yet, since *therto* probably means here 'in addition,' 'moreover,' we should expect what follows to be different from what went before.

51–56. The battles in ll. 51 and 56–66 were of Christians against the Muslims, and were all in the Mediterranean area. Those in ll. 54–55 were of Christians against the heathen of N.E. Europe.

Granada (56) was occupied by the Arabs during the earlier Middle Ages, and *Algezir*, the modern Algeciras, near Gibraltar, was their gateway from Africa; it was captured by a European army in 1344. *Tramissene* (62) and *Belmarye* (57) were Arab provinces in N. Africa opposite Spain, from which they left for Europe, but to what campaigns against them Chaucer is referring we do not know exactly.

Campaigns at the east end of the Mediterranean were led by Peter, King of Cyprus, who visited England in 1363 on a recruiting campaign. He captured *Satalye* (58), the modern Adalia on the coast of Turkey north-west of Cyprus, in 1361; *Lieis* (58), the modern Ayas, then the chief port of Armenia, was temporarily captured in 1367; and likewise, in 1365, Alexandria (51), one of the richest and best defended strongholds of the Sultan.

By *Palatye* (65) is probably meant modern Palatia, on the west coast of Turkey, opposite the island of Patmos, and the *lord* of it may have been a heathen who had made a friendly agreement with King Peter of Cyprus, as some did, and who was therefore helped against *another hethen* (66) in Turkey.

The Grete See (59) is probably the Mediterranean, or the eastern end of it.

Against *Lettow* (54), the modern Lithuania, and *Ruce* (54) or Russia, the Knight would have fought with the Teutonic Knights. 'To begin the board' (52) was to be given the place of honour at any banqueting table. Originally, when the host sat at the end, looking down the length of the table, the honourable place at his right hand was the first on the long side, and so 'began the table.' When the fashion changed and the host moved to the centre of the long side, the expression was still applied to the honourable place on his right. Chaucer may be referring particularly to a banqueting ceremonial of the Teutonic Knights in which foreign knights were placed in order of precedence at table by the heralds.

75–76. The *habergeoun* was the coat of mail, in Chaucer's time ending at the hips. Plate armour covered arms and legs, also the chest, above the coat of mail.

By the *gypoun* Chaucer may mean, perhaps, an outer garment, a tight-fitting vest worn immediately over the mail and breastplate and also ending at the hips, or, perhaps, a garment worn under the mail. The portrait in the Ellesmere MS., however, shows the Knight wearing a full-sleeved and loose garment, reaching to the knee.

79. THE SQUIRE. The Knight represents the religious ideal of the medieval gentleman, but the Squire represents that of the lover (80). He delights in living with refined intensity, loving with such ardour that he cannot sleep a wink (97–98), dressed in the height of young gentlemen's fashion in the reign of King Richard II (93), his clothes and his spirit gaily ornamented, the first with embroidered flowers (89–90), the second with such accomplishments as jousting, dancing, and drawing (96). But he is no affected fop, and is as 'fresh' as the

spring with which Chaucer opened the Prologue (92); the colours he is dressed in are simple—white and red (90); he is an athlete (84), and a horseman (94), and sings all day with spontaneous joy (91).

Whereas the Squire is above all filled with *joie de vivre*, the Knight is somewhat ascetic. But the Knight is getting on in years, whereas the Squire is a young man, and this made all the difference to what was expected of them. It was a common literary theme that youth is the proper time for the gay lover with spring in the heart and in the world about, but age for the penitent preparing to meet his Maker.

The Squire does all he can to win the favour of his loved-one, and even his campaigning has been in the hope of securing her admiration, and, as a consequence, 'his lady's merciful favour' (88). In the medieval literature of love the man often spoke of the woman in terms more appropriate to the veneration of the Blessed Virgin, and the service of his feudal lord. That is why she is called his 'lady.' A young aspirant to knighthood (80), he has fought in wars near at home only, and only for his lady, not for Christ.

He is an honourable servant of his father's, and always humbly eager to be of service, his principal office being to wait at his lord's table (99–100). He would serve literally 'in front of' his father, who would sit with other diners on one side of a long table while his squire carved facing him on the other. In this hard but honourable way he learned 'courtesy' (99), and was 'well bred' (see THE KNIGHT).

Chaucer had himself served as a young man, perhaps a squire, in the army of Edward III which marched from Calais to Rheims in 1359 through Flanders, Artois, and Picardy. He, too, had served in great households, and had written songs, especially about love. He wrote also of two other squires in the Merchant's Tale and Franklin's Tale, but though it is likely that to some hearers of these stories about Damian and Aurelius these squires were in some respects ridiculous, in the Prologue Chaucer is not satirizing the young gallant any more than he satirized his sober and religious father, the Knight. At only one point might we suspect a quiet smile, and that is at his lack of sleep (97–98).

At the same time the differences in technique between this portrait and that of the Knight are notable. The latter is built in three blocks with a tail-piece about outward appearance. It is simple and orderly. But the description of the Squire darts from his hair to his age to his stature to his war-service to his love and so on.

85–86. English armies invaded these provinces in 1359 (see THE SQUIRE), and in 1383, when a raid was headed by the Bishop of Norwich ostensibly against the French supporters of the antipope Clement, and in favour of Urban VI of Rome. England then held Calais, which made these three provinces very vulnerable.

95. 'He knew how to compose songs and to write well,' *make* probably referring to the music of the song, and *endite* to the words.

101. THE YEOMAN. Caxton's *The Book of the Ordre of Chivalry* (*E.E.T.S.*, O.S. 168, p. 19), a translation of a French book to be found in a manuscript about contemporary with Chaucer, says, "the highe honour whiche longeth to a knight" requires "that there be given to him a squier and servaun that may take hede to his horse." His dignity ought to be supported by attendants, but Chaucer says of his Knight (*he*, 101) that he preferred going on his pilgrimage with a yeoman only. He is not a gentleman for extravagant show.

'Yeoman' was, like 'squire' in some of its uses, a title of service in a great household, ranking below a squire and above a groom, and generally an assistant to a higher official. The service might be indoors or out, and, like another yeoman in the Friar's Tale who is an estate bailiff, the Knight's yeoman is not an indoor attendant but a sort of keeper from his estate, probably charged with protecting the wild beasts which all medieval gentlemen loved to hunt. Chaucer himself was once deputy forester of a royal estate in Somerset and doubtless had many such men as the Yeoman in his service there.

115. A small image of St Christopher (perhaps martyred by the Emperor Decius somewhere in Asia Minor in A.D. 250). It was believed that whoever looked on his face should not that day suffer sudden death, and his picture, therefore, was very common in the Middle Ages, especially painted on walls of churches immediately opposite the door or at bridges. The legend says he carried travellers across a raging river for God's sake, being of enormous stature, and one day carried a child on his shoulder who weighed him down so much that it seemed he was carrying the weight of the whole world. The child was Jesus.

118. THE PRIORESS. A Prioress was either the head or the deputy head of a convent of nuns, that is to say, women who have given themselves up for ever to a life of perfection, possessing all things in common, entirely obedient to their spiritual superior, the Prioress, and perpetually chaste. So that they may suffer fewer temptations they are required to remain inside the walls of their convent, cut off from the world. Such, at least, are the requirements of the Rule of St Benedict (see THE MONK); and such injunctions as the Papal Bull *Periculoso* at the end of the thirteenth century forbade all nuns to leave their convents on any pretext whatsoever. Various bishops forbade nuns in their diocese to wear the head-veil high off the forehead, or to use ornaments.

But as we do not know to what extent Chaucer was acquainted with the rules that should have guided the life of a prioress as a religious, we cannot be sure that he knew a nun was forbidden all jewellery; and unless we know this we cannot say that when he describes a brooch on the person of this nun he intends us to think not only of what she is, but also of what she ought to be. We cannot be sure that Chaucer is suggesting, even most delicately, that, as her vocation demands, she ought to love God and not ornaments.

Moreover, we do not know to what extent Chaucer was acquainted with the minor variety of practice in nunneries which was officially allowed by different visiting bishops. St Benedict said nothing about the keeping of pets. Some bishops said that nuns might keep a dog, some strictly forbade it.

It is generally assumed that Chaucer refers to the breadth of the Prioress's forehead as an oblique comment on the fact that any forehead was showing at all. Her wimple should have covered it completely down to her eyes according to several bishops' injunctions. But in contemporary pictures with no satirical intention nuns often have their foreheads uncovered, and it may well be that Chaucer, like these nuns, did not think this exact requirement important. He may not have known of it, and when he talks of her forehead he may be referring quite simply to its breadth. This interpretation is supported by l. 156.

Throughout the description Chaucer is in the first place presenting a medieval *lady*. In the second place he is describing a medieval *nun*. The first four lines set this key for the whole. L. 119 uses the unmistakable language of polite medieval literature, and it describes the Prioress as if she were the heroine of a Romance. Such a lady was conventionally *simple and coy*, not 'exotic, ingenuous, unaffected, in disposition or facial expression,' and 'becomingly quiet.' Ideally, she had the Prioress's shapely nose, vivacious eyes, tiny red mouth, broad forehead (152–155), and her smile. The fastidious daintiness of her table-manners (127–136) is a clear mark of her good breeding.

Most nuns were of gentle birth, or, at the least, the daughters of rich merchants and guildsmen. At least locally a prioress would be regarded as one of the great ladies of the region. Her family ties and her administration of the convent estates alone would keep all but the holiest in constant touch with upper-class society, especially in the neighbourhood of London.

But Chaucer suggests in several lines a self-conscious excess of gentility. This is clear in her imitation of the ways of court and her endeavour to be worthy of deference (139–141). There is some incongruity in the aspirations of a lady who, because of her vocation, cannot be of the court, to act as if

she were. Elegant misperformance is suggested by her gen-
teel speaking of a French never spoken in France, and possibly
by her singing (122–123).

Perhaps the key to the Prioress is Chaucer's use of *semely*
(see Glossary) three times in describing her, whereas he uses
it on one other occasion only in the whole of the Prologue,
and never so consistently of one character anywhere else in his
other poems.

There is ample ironic scope in a character who is a lady and
at the same time a nun. But the irony becomes the more
subtle when we realize that in many medieval writers the
world of romance, which turned about the Lady, shaded into
the world of religion. Modern parallels to this are seen in the
saying, "Cleanliness is next to godliness," or in the idea that,
all other things being equal, a gentleman is a better Christian
than a man with no social graces. There is nothing excep-
tional in this aspect of the Prioress. It is in the subtlety with
which Chaucer has shaded the one world into the other that
his creation is unique. For he has presented several features
of the Prioress in such a way that in one light they are those
of a religious, but in another they are those of a lady. (*Cf.* THE
KNIGHT.) Thus the Prioress wears a brooch inscribed 'Love
overcomes all.' There could be no more suitable motto for
a religious. But it is a quotation from Vergil's *Eclogue* x, 69
and it would have a different meaning for the Squire, who
could not sleep a wink for the other sort of love referred to
there. The subtlety, however, is this: though, fundamentally,
Christian love and sexual love are something very different,
superficially in the Middle Ages they could be very like (*cf.*
THE SQUIRE and THE KNIGHT).

There is also play on the ambiguity of the word *conscience*
(142) for it means not only that moral sensitivity, the inner
recognition of right and wrong, which is its exclusively
modern meaning, and which in a nun should be near per-
fection, but also that general tenderness of feeling which
characterized the ideal medieval lady, what Jane Austen
would have called 'sensibility.' Thus the Prioress sentiment-

ally lavishes love on lap-dogs, not men. Her confessor would charge her with trying to be a lady and not a nun; but the Prioress would say that she was practising religion like the lady she ought to be.

120. The Prioress probably swears by St Loy because his name is pleasant on the tongue, and because he was famed for his beauty, craftsmanship, and courtesy. St Eligius, Eloi, or Loy lived in the seventh century and rose from goldsmith's apprentice to Master of the Mint of the king of France. After exercising much influence in the court, he became a priest, renounced his wealth and position, and ultimately as Bishop of Noyon evangelized much of Flanders.

121. *Eglentine* means 'sweet-briar' and is in itself a pleasant name for a sweetly disposed lady. It is also a name given to ladies in medieval romances. But Argentyne and Idoine, the latter also the name of a lady in an actual romance, were names of nuns to whom Elizabeth of Hainaut left gifts in her will. Thus Chaucer may be using the name innocently, knowing actual nuns had names like it, or may be making a private allusion to such a nun, or perhaps asking us to smile because such names are romantic and not pious.

122–123. Many religious each day offer to God eight services of prayers, psalms, hymns, and readings from the Scriptures. These compose the 'Divine Office,' and are called 'Hours' because they are done at eight particular hours of the day and night. They would be sung in church by the Prioress and her nuns.

Chanting tends to become nasal unless the singers are very good, and the fault is so common that it is unlikely that Chaucer regards the Prioress as exceptionally amusing just for singing in her nose. But since it is often due to a sort of inhibition preventing the wide opening of the mouth, or to untrained reliance on the nose for controlling the strength of the noise rather than on chest and diaphragm, it is possible to see in it scope for humour at the expense of the Prioress in particular. There is often a genteel sanctity in the reediness of nasal intonation; but the joke may be in the Prioress's sensing the indelicacy of nasal noises and therefore making them with as much delicacy as can be.

124–125. See THE PRIORESS. For three hundred years before Chaucer a form of French had been spoken by the upper class in England as their first language. It was not the French spoken in Paris, and the use of it was going out of fashion in Chaucer's time, so that it may be by speaking it that the Prioress gives amusement. What is more likely, however, is this: there was a convent dedicated to St Leonard at Stratford atte Bow, now Stratford le Bow or just Bow, in East London, but then two and a half miles beyond the city walls. At this convent one of the nuns had been Elizabeth of Hainaut, sister of Queen Philippa, wife of King Edward III. The French spoken in Hainaut, what is now southern Belgium, was then probably no nearer Parisian French than it is to-day. So that French 'according to the school of Stratford' may be a private allusion to the particular pronunciation of members of the royal family and, perhaps, of Chaucer's own wife, who also probably came from Hainaut.

152. The meaning of *greye* (see Glossary), and the significance of the comparison with *glas* are not known precisely.

159. A set of beads, a rosary, with its 'gauds' of green. A rosary nowadays is a string of beads arranged in fifteen groups of eleven beads each, the last bead (the 'gaud') in each group being larger than the other ten. A 'Hail Mary' is said at each of the ten small beads and then an 'Our Father' at each large, and at each of these decades one of the mysteries of the Redemption is meditated.

163–164. Although the second nun is not described here or any-where else, she is one of the tellers of tales. She is the Prior-ess's chaplain, perhaps her personal assistant and secretary, perhaps simply a travelling companion, for nuns may not travel alone.

The three priests make a difficulty which is discussed in the Introduction, pp. 16–17.

165. THE MONK. A monk is one who should be following the Way of Perfection which Jesus Christ counselled the young

man in Matthew xix, 16 ff. He should have renounced all material pleasures and possessions, and, in a life of supervised self-denial, be seeking only spiritual welfare.

St Benedict was the father of monasticism in the western world. He was the creator of a Rule or code of conduct governing the lives of monks at every hour of the day. It requires the religious to be a member of one community which he is never to leave, and in which he is to live a communal life of unvarying routine, devoting some four hours of every day to liturgical prayer (see note, ll. 122–123), four more to meditative reading and private prayer, and six or more to crafts, domestic duties, or manual labour. St Benedict emphasized the part such work should play in the religious life, but it is unlikely that the monks ever went every day in a body to cultivate the fields. Certainly in Chaucer's day the Benedictine or Black Monks (black being the colour of their dress) lived on what was grown by the unaided efforts of the ordinary country labourers settled on the lands with which the pious laity had endowed the monastery.

Through such generosity, and skilful, sometimes selfish, management, Benedictine monasteries had become great corporate landowners. This was, perhaps, the greatest of all the dangers to their religious life. The superiors of these opulent houses, the abbots, originally intended by St Benedict to be primarily fathers of a spiritual family, had become powers in the land, and at home lived in special and luxurious quarters. This is the rôle Chaucer has in mind in l. 167.

Since monastic lands might be scattered over several counties an inevitable practice grew up of administering the remote parts from *cells* detached from the main house. There were sometimes other reasons for their existence, but they were generally small settlements of one to a half-dozen monks. The separation from the mother house reduced discipline, and religion became tepid. It was always a good excuse for living outside the cloister and Chaucer's Monk is typically the head of one of these cells (172).

He is an 'outrider' (166), a religious specially permitted to

leave the cloister because he is an officer of the convent
attending to its external domestic requirements and especially
to its estates. Dealing as he did with such wealth, such an
officer easily forgot his ascetic calling and played the great
lord as he rode from farm to farm.

It is difficult to decide where Chaucer's enthusiastic amuse-
ment at the Monk as a man of distinguished personality
ends, and that at the incongruity of his ideal and actual life
begins. He largely repeats features described in the bitter
satires of earlier and contemporary writers, but the relish
with which he does so is unprecedented. Instead of the pale
and wasted look of the ascetic who will make no compromise
with the world, this Monk has the dignified spread of the
higher-ranking cleric (204). Chaucer revels in this picture as
much as the Monk revels in his swan.

165. *for the maistrye* is an adverbial phrase limiting *fair*. Thus, 'a
really fine one' (see Glossary).

173. According to the *Dialogues* of St Gregory (*c.* 540–604) St
Benedict (480–?543) was the son of a nobleman and grew up
in Rome, but early in life he retired to the mountains as a
hermit, eventually founding at Monte Cassino the monastery
in which he probably composed his Rule and where it was
probably first practised.

St Maurus was a disciple of St Benedict and was said to
have introduced the Benedictine Rule into France in 543,
founding an abbey at Glanfeuil.

173–176. The sentence begun in l. 173 is broken off at the end
of l. 174. Ll. 175–176 probably mean, 'This monk we're
talking of had no truck with out-of-date practices, and fol-
lowed the way of the new fashion.'

177–178. A comment (attributed to St Jerome) on Psalm xc, 3,
in the Vulgate (xci in the Authorized Version) explaining the
'trap of the huntsman,' says that there are many huntsmen
who seek after our souls, and that Nimrod (Genesis x, 9) and
Esau (Genesis xxvii, 3) were hunters and sinners, "et penitus
non invenimus in Scripturis Sanctis, sanctum aliquem vena-
torem"—'and we do not find anywhere in the Scriptures one
holy hunter.'

In his *City of God* (xvi, 4) St Augustine explains that the reference to Nimrod in Genesis x, 9 is wrongly translated and should not read '*before* the Lord' but '*against* the Lord'; and, says St Augustine, 'what is the word hunter but an entrapper, persecutor, and murderer of earthly creatures?'

In the first effective systematization of canon law by Gratian in the twelfth century, bishops, priests, and deacons are forbidden to keep dogs or hawks for hunting and to go roaming the forests as hunters because of the din and impossibility of thinking about divine matters on a hunt. Fishing, on the other hand, is quite permissible.

Hunting was, however, the great sport of gentlemen, and that is why this 'lord,' who looks so much more like a gentleman than a monk, practises it. He should have eschewed all worldly comforts and ornaments (193–197 and 203).

179–181. A commonplace comparison probably deriving from Gratian (see note, ll. 177–178).

185. The cloisters formed the library of a monastery, and each monk had a reading-desk in a window. But sober *clerical* pursuits are not interesting to this 'modern' monk who prefers to be a gentleman.

187. St Augustine (354–430) spent his youth in N. Africa, where he became a brilliant student and then teacher of rhetoric. In 383 he went to Italy, and, after a spiritual crisis recorded in his *Confessions*, he was baptized by Ambrose in 387 at Milan. Ordained priest in 391 and consecrated bishop in 396, he combined pastoral duties and an austere communal life with his clergy, all bound to religious poverty.

Many bodies of religious professed obedience to a Rule supposedly composed by St Augustine, but, in fact, concocted in the late eleventh century from separate works, really written by him, a letter, a sermon, and a treatise *De Opere Monachorum*, which concern communal religious life. It was especially in the last of these three that St Augustine bade the able-bodied religious to do manual work in imitation of St Paul (186), for the gifts of the faithful should be reserved for those who cannot work.

187. *How shal the world be served?* The question is probably

meant to suggest a 'progressive' man who feels it wrong to cut himself off in a cloister from the world that needs his services, while being only too eager to enjoy all the material advantages of a monastic life in the later Middle Ages.

202. '[eyes] which gleamed like the fire under a cauldron.'

208. THE FRIAR. The Friar's affected lisp (264–265) and the mention of his name (269) need not be signs that Chaucer had a particular friar in mind. They are the means by which Chaucer gives individuality to a character many features of which are found elsewhere. For example, 'False-seeming,' an allegorical figure in the *Romaunt of the Rose* (ll. 6135–7696 in Chaucer's translation), pretends, as a friar, to poverty, but befriends only the rich, confesses all comers by special papal privilege, and meddles in legal matters. The *Romaunt*, however, does not present one hypocritical person but a series of hypocritical traits. These are colourful, but they compose a shapeless list. Chaucer presents a unique human being.

The friars, unlike monks, submitted themselves to corporate as well as individual poverty, and unlike monks their vocation was in the secular world, preaching and administering the sacraments. They lived on alms, and are therefore referred to as the Mendicants. Few can have lived lives more like Christ's than a truly fervent friar.

There were numerous orders, but only four main ones (210). A good mnemonic is the name CAIM (Cain) by which the satirists of the Middle Ages abused them. Chaucer does not indicate to which order this Friar belongs.

(1) Carmelites, or 'White' friars (from their dress), were initially hermits (or solitary recluses) living on the slopes of Mount Carmel in Palestine, and they received their Rule, a very strict one, about 1210. But in 1229 they became a mendicant, or begging, order and spread through Europe.

(2) Austin friars. In the first half of the thirteenth century there were many small groups of hermits in central Italy, and these were organized about 1250 by Pope Innocent IV into an Order following the so-called Rule of St Augustine (see note, l. 187). They wore black.

(3) Iacobini (from the *rue Jacobin* in Paris where they had a house), the Dominicans or 'Black' friars, grew out of St Dominic's preaching mission against the Albigensian heretics in the early thirteenth century, and were established in 1215. They were especially learned in scholastic theology (St Thomas Aquinas himself was one of them), and were important members of the Universities which had begun to grow up in the century before their foundation.

(4) Minorites, the Franciscans, or 'Grey' friars. St Francis lived the life of complete poverty, humility, and perfect charity. The Pope had formally recognized his disciples by 1210, but the organization into an 'order' in 1220 was contrary to St Francis' initial intention, which was purely evangelical. The new Order, however, evangelized in the growing cities.

It was not long before the Franciscans followed the Dominicans to the Universities (Duns Scotus, for example, was a Franciscan), and from the middle of the thirteenth century, the great century of the friars, most of the leading theologians and philosophers were members of one or other of these two great mendicant orders.

The friars appear to have traded on this reputation, and were, indeed, often more learned than a parish priest. Doubtless, however, many were ignorant; and medieval satirists certainly play on their pretension to the proud title, 'Master of Arts' or 'Master of Divinity' (261), which was inconsistent with their vow of humility. They should have been humble like a "poure scoler" (260) such as the Clerk of Oxford, if one at all. Great dignity attached to the degree of Master, which was a 'solemn' status in the sense in which Chaucer calls the Friar a 'solemn' man (see note l. 209), and on being received into the corporation of teachers a scholar was expected to give lavish feasts appropriate to his new dignity. In the Summoner's Tale (D 2185–2188) a friar unctuously refuses the title of 'master,' though entitled to it, on the grounds that Jesus forbade it (Matthew xxiii, 8, and Mark x, 43–44).

The friars were under papal protection and control; and fearing, therefore, no local authority, they tended to abuse their privileges. A papal bull of 1281 (*Ad fructus uberes*) modified by one of 1311 (*Super cathedram*) had given the friars power to hear confessions throughout a diocese without the agreement of parish priests, provided that they had obtained a licence to do so from the bishop, who was compelled to license a certain number (220). Those who, like this Friar, had the licence, are sometimes criticized for advertising themselves as confessors who could give absolution from more serious sins than the parish priest. Friar Hubert adds, as an extra attraction, the imposition of particularly easy penances (223), or works of atonement in token satisfaction for sin forgiven by Christ, and is, indeed, ready to accept money as the condition of his absolution instead of a contrite heart (231–232). In this way he plays on the credulity of his penitents because for the sacrament of penance are necessary not only confession, but also contrition and satisfaction, and without contrition there is no forgiveness.

He is a *limitour* (209), that is to say, his convent has assigned him an area of certain 'limits' in which to beg on its behalf. Ll. 252 b and c suggest that such a privileged beggar paid a fixed sum to the convent, was protected from competition, and, presumably, kept what he won over and above his *ferme* for himself.

Itinerant friars clearly made admirable pedlars (233–234). But it may be that Chaucer implies that the knick-knacks Friar Hubert carries are to be given away as attractive bait to those women for whom ultimately (Chaucer probably suggests in ll. 212–213) he arranges marriages with proper husbands. This he would do by offering with them an attractive dowry, the proceeds of his hypocritical begging. There is evidence in contemporary moralists and in historical records of both the peddling and the seducing friar.

208–211. One sense of *wantowne* is 'merry' and 'gay.' Thus the Friar lisps as an attractive 'whim' or 'caprice' (264). His *wantownesse* is again shown in his merry singing (235), and his general sportiveness. *Wantowne* also has the modern sense of 'lascivious,' and this aspect of the Friar may be suggested in ll. 210–213. The basic sense of the word is 'undisciplined,' 'unrestrained.'

Daliaunce also has two senses. The innocent one is simply 'conversation,' either light or serious. The second is 'amorous play,' and it grows out of the first because cultivated conversation was regarded as one of the most important features of making love in the Middle Ages. In ll. 210–211 Chaucer may be playing on both senses of the word.

209. *Solempne* is etymologically connected with established festivals, and means 'connected with religious rites,' 'formal,' 'ceremonious,' 'sumptuous,' 'imposing.' To call a man 'solemn' in Chaucer's time did not mean he was grave and earnest. Those are precisely the qualities of the Clerk of Oxford and the Parish Priest, but the word is never used of them. Indeed, it is said of the latter that he "waited after no pomp and reverence" (525). That is just what the Friar loves (259–261).

227–228. 'For if a man gave, the Friar would make so bold as to say he knew for sure that the man was repentant.'

233. The Friar's *tipet* is probably the elongated pointed end of his hood which he has thrown back off his head and which is hanging down his shoulders. But the word can also mean a long band or tube of cloth hanging from a sleeve (*cf.* that on the gown of a Master of Arts), or a garment covering the shoulders like a cape. The illustration in the Ellesmere MS. shows a hood.

240–251. The irony of these lines arises from the Friar's turning to his own ends the ambiguity of some respectable words, and from the fact that he of all men, in theory devoted to a life of poverty and charity, ought to have been the last to use such arguments. Chaucer appears to find its witty depiction more amusing than he finds the hypocrisy morally wrong. The wit is in the words *honeste* (246), *avaunce* (246), and *profit* (249) (*cf. conscience* and *love* in THE PRIORESS).

254. St John's gospel begins, "*In principio erat verbum*," 'In the

beginning was the Word,' and doubtless the Friar recited the first fourteen verses. These compose the last gospel at mass in the modern western church when there is no proper last gospel, a custom obtaining at least from the Missal (1570) of Pius V. In the Middle Ages, when few could read, the words were often used, especially by friars, who recited them for money, as if they had a magical effect.

256. Probably proverbial. His income was cunningly derived from irregular odds and ends, and was not a steady and proper one. Of course, no friar had a steady income.

258. *lovedayes*, settlements of legal disputes out of court. Originally such a settlement was amicable to avoid the ill-feeling of a judicial decision, and was held on a day appointed by the court trying the case. The Friar, however, who attends such meetings scolding (257) with the demeanour of a lordly scholar and prelate, and without healing humility and poverty (259–263), shows the corruption of the practice, for he enjoys his temporary rôle as arbiter, and overawes the poorer disputants, perhaps in favour of the richer who paid him to do so.

263. The Friar's cloak is clearly so ample that it falls like a rounded bell from his shoulders to the ground. *out of the presse* may mean 'when newly taken out of the clothes cupboard' (*i.e.* trim and stiff), or 'when taken out of the clothes press' where it has been pressed into shape.

270. THE MERCHANT is a wholesale exporter and importer as is implied by ll. 276–277. He keeps up prosperous appearances by the imposing conduct of his complicated business (281–282), and by using his brains (279), but in actual fact he is in debt (280). The emphasis is on his single-minded, rather self-important, interest in business and business only. Chaucer's friend, John Gower, in his *Mirour de l'homme* (25813 ff.), comments on merchants who contracted great debts which they could not repay, in order to keep up inflated appearances, and describes (7225 ff.) how usurers exploited the financial needs of knights and squires, practising on them 'what is called in the modern phrase "chevisance of money".' In Chaucer's

age such merchants as the one he describes were newly becoming powers in the land, for kings borrowed from them to finance wars and alliances. Many orthodox and aristocratic moralists were fiercely rude at their expense. They would have said that this Merchant's restless 'busyness' was stimulated by the sin of avarice and was the very opposite of that *fredom*, or disregard for money, characteristic of a true gentleman. (See THE KNIGHT.) But Chaucer sees it as just one more colourful aspect of a particular human being, and as enjoyably ironic—for the Merchant is all the while in debt!

This irony is an end in itself and is not used to make the Merchant a more arresting moral object-lesson. But even so, though in such a difference between appearance and intention on one side and real achievement on the other there is scope for the intensest irony, the temperature rises scarcely more than in the use of *estatly* in l. 281, where if there is wit at all it is of the quietest and least aggressive.

The Merchant makes money in the black market by foreign exchange (278). The law then, as now, required him, for example, to sell for English currency the French money he received from his French customers through the money-changers appointed by the King and not at unofficial offices and unofficial rates.

The Merchant may belong to one or both of two great English organizations, the Merchants of the Staple, and the Merchant Adventurers. The Merchants of the Staple exported primarily wool (England's great 'staple' article of commerce) and hides, and at different times certain towns in England and on the Continent were specified as the only ones through which the business could be done. This was a means of government control to facilitate the collection of customs. From 1383 to 1388 Middelburg (277) was one of these towns. It is a small Dutch town on the island of Walcheren in the estuary of the Scheldt, on which river stands Antwerp, and is due east of Orwell (277), a port now under the sea but then standing at the mouth of the River Orwell on which lies Ipswich. Flanders (272) is the country between the Scheldt estuary and modern France, the western part, that is, of modern Belgium. Wool imported from England was woven at Ypres, Ghent, and Bruges into cloth (see THE WIFE OF BATH).

The Merchant Adventurers resided in foreign cities and imported the cloth made in England from English wool. Eventually the exports of cloth far exceeded that of wool. The Adventurers used Middelburg as their headquarters from 1384 on; and this, or the fact that it was one of the specified marketing towns may explain why Chaucer mentions it in particular.

Chaucer had relations who were wine merchants, and while himself Controller of Customs must have associated daily with such men as the Merchant.

276. Pirates and French privateers would be the Merchant's nightmare. It was the king's right and duty to guard the English seas, and this he did by farming the task out to private individuals—for there was then no navy—who were paid by special taxes on merchandise (tunnage and poundage).

285. THE CLERK. Chaucer uses the word *clerk* with the predominant sense of 'learned man,' a sense which grew out of (but did not supplant) the original meaning, 'cleric,' because in medieval christendom the clergy were almost exclusively the learned men. Legally, a 'clerk' was not necessarily a learned man at all, but essentially one in some way connected with the service of the Church, usually in orders, and distinguished by the tonsure and specially sober dress. Such men could not be tried in civil courts of law, but only in ecclesiastical. At the University of Oxford it seems to have been assumed that all students were *ipso facto* clerks.

A student at Oxford in Chaucer's day would probably take four years to get his B.A. degree, and another three or four for his M.A. Logic (286) would in all probability be studied in both parts of the course, though the text-books for the M.A. would be more difficult. This second part of the course probably also included much philosophy, natural, moral, and metaphysical, and for this Aristotle provided the tools: so that the emphasis on Aristotle and his philosophy in l. 295, together with the mention of logic in l. 286, may mean the Clerk has 'for long proceeded with his studies for the M.A.' His apparent readiness, however, for a benefice (291) cannot be taken as a sure pointer to his academic standing, for many gained benefices without a degree at all. Moreover, though the course for both B.A. and M.A. included many subjects, one subject tended to predominate; so that, if, as is probable, logic predominated in the Oxford of Chaucer's day, Chaucer may have used the subject 'logic' to stand for the Arts course in general, and he may simply mean that the Clerk had long been a university man.

By 'logic' itself, Chaucer means the science of reasoning, the way one argues. Medieval scholars were all examined orally, and had to maintain or dispute a thesis (or 'motion' as it might not altogether improperly be called in the language of the modern debating society).

The philosophy of Aristotle (384–322 B.C.) was known to medieval Europe from the twelfth century in Latin translations of Arabic translations of the original Greek—a way in which much ancient learning was saved for an age largely ignorant of Greek—and from the thirteenth century increasingly in direct translation from Greek to Latin. Though he wrote on ethics, politics, rhetoric, and logic, Aristotle's attention seems to have been markedly to the empirical and scientific, for he wrote about many aspects of the physical universe. At first the Church had been suspicious of these ideas (especially those about the nature of matter and about metaphysics) which poured into Europe from the pre-Christian ancient world; but by Chaucer's time they had on the whole been assimilated by the scholastic philosophers, such as St Thomas Aquinas, into one consistent picture of the material and spiritual creation.

The Clerk refuses merely secular jobs which an ecclesiastic ought not to perform (292), unlike many actual clerics of his day—for example, the Monk (187), who delighted to serve the world in its administrative offices. Such clerks either

skimped or left entirely undone their priestly duties and
became civil servants or stewards to great lords. Such jobs
paid well and ultimately brought ecclesiastical preferment.
Wiclif, for example, complained that it was not the good clerk
who was presented to livings but "a kitchen clerk or a pen
clerk or [one] wise of building of castles or worldly doing,
though he cannot read well his psalter and knows not the
commandments of God nor sacraments of the Holy Church."

The usual means of providing for university students was
the patronage of their local bishop, monastery, or great lord,
or of a number of 'friends' (299), because to give alms
for education is a pious act. In all probability the Clerk will
not be from a family of the lowest and poorest class, but the
son of a yeoman, merchant, craftsman, or even a gentleman.

The description of the clerk has an unwonted continuity,
and none of the more usual light leaping from one dissimilar
to another. It is tidied off with a line sober and unaffected,
which, in these respects, as in its meaning, neatly sums up the
whole character.

294. *blak or reed*, a tag which probably means 'any colour,' so
that the bindings are not exclusively of these two colours.

297–298. A pun. A philosopher was:

(1) a man of wisdom, devoted to the search for funda-
mental truth as to-day, but also possessing systematic know-
ledge of the physical universe, of metaphysics, and of ethics;

(2) a special sort of philosopher in sense (1), an alchemist, or
misguided seeker for the 'philosopher's stone,' a substance
which would restore all things to their youth and turn all
metals into gold.

306. 'Concise, acute, and packed with solid sense.' He wasted no
words either on frivolous subjects or rhetorical ornaments.

307. 'What he said had always some connexion with virtue.'
Moral vertu is a rendering of Aristotle's term for 'excellence
of character' as distinguished from intellectual 'virtue' or
'excellence.'

309. THE SERJEANT AT LAW. A barrister at the very top of his
tree. Serjeants at Law, or *servientes ad legem*, were the King's

legal servants. The office was abolished in 1880. It was filled by barristers who had spent at least sixteen years in the general study of the law, and the status and eminence conferred by the honour of this promotion was no less than that accompanying the degree of Doctor in a university. The new Serjeant, like the new Doctor or Master, had to spend much on feasting and gifts to support the dignity of his new rank, but he could soon reimburse himself, for only Serjeants could plead in the Court of Common Bench, where all pleas of real property were heard.

Many of Chaucer's contemporaries complained of the lawyers' lining their pockets by exploiting the necessities of their clients and especially of the poor. By the wealth they had won with their legal skill lawyers were enabled to rival the established lords and gentlemen in the ownership of land and the status that went with it. They were *nouveaux riches*, and unacceptable as such. But Chaucer as usual makes no raw diatribes and violent accusations. He mentions some of the causes for others' complaints about lawyers, but treats these causes altogether differently: his Serjeant is an impressively shrewd and competent man (320 and 323 ff.), but with plenty of window-dressing; and it is not the public misrepresentation of justice or the breach of law with impunity which enlivens Chaucer's pen, but the comparatively harmless characteristics of *appearing* a reverend figure because his utterances are so wise, and *appearing* busier than he actually is.

Thus Chaucer refers to his skilful investment of his earnings in land (318-320) without any obvious irony in his tone. Wiclif makes it clear what Chaucer means by these lines when he says that lawyers "get them gold and purchase rents and lands of lords and destroy very [true] heirs; and this destroys much our land. For how should right be among such men that this day have but their penny, and anon purchase rents and lands to be peers with knights or barons? . . . Thus lords and other men [have] for this falseness to hold them at fees and other great costs, for else with their wiles and falseness they will drive lords and gentlemen out of their

houses, heritage, and all their goods. . . . And though it be
bought openly against the law, yet by cavillings these lawyers
hold it forth, that the rightful heir may as well buy a strange
lordship as get his own." The Serjeant not only acquires
land by means other than inheritance (*purchasen*), for example,
by buying it, but also acquires unrestricted possession of it
(*fee simple*), getting round by his legal skill any entail re-
stricting the estate to certain heirs and made his title defective
(*infect*).

Sometimes a Serjeant had a temporary commission to go on
circuit as judge in assize (314): that is to say, though not a
permanent judge but a barrister pleading before the judges of
the Courts of Common Law, he was sometimes specially
appointed by an open letter of the King (315), and with a
commission giving him full power to hear all cases (315), to
act as judge in courts held periodically in the counties.

310. *Parvis* is probably derived from *paradisum*, and may mean
'an area in front of the door of a church,' for example, at old
St Paul's, London. There is no evidence that this space was
used by lawyers, though the word *parvis* is certainly elsewhere
connected with the law. But there exists a description of a
ceremony in 1577–78 when old Serjeants led newly appointed
Serjeants each to a pillar *inside* St Paul's. It is added that the
ceremony is ancient and that formerly Serjeants heard their
clients' cases at their own pillars. If it is to this old custom
that Chaucer is referring, then the Serjeant will have been
often at the *Parvis*, either as an old member, to instal new
men, which supplements the picture of his venerability, or to
hear many clients' cases, which supplements the picture of
great activity.

317. It was common in the Middle Ages to remunerate not only
with money but also with suits of clothes.

323–324. This claim cannot be taken literally. The Year Books,
or unofficial records of cases, do not seem to have been com-
posed earlier than the time of Edward I, two centuries after
William I, and the Plea Rolls, or official records, were, as
such, kept in official custody, and a Serjeant could not consult
them except for special reasons.

331. THE FRANKLIN. This description is in three main parts. The longest—half the whole—concerns his liberal housekeeping (339–354), and the last refers to his part in local and national government (355–360). It is in these features that the Franklin contrasts with the Knight. In many cases franklins were substantial landed gentlemen. Sir John Fortescue, writing, about 1470, of the flourishing face of England, said that it is "so well stocked and replete with possessors of land and fields, that in it no hamlet, however small, can be found in which there is no knight, esquire, or householder of the sort commonly called a franklin [miles, armiger, vel paterfamilias qualis ibidem frankeleyn vulgariter nuncupatur] well-off in possessions; nor numerous other free tenants and many yeomen." In John Russell's list of precedence, composed about 1440, franklins, serjeants at law, and squires are placed together, and, of course, below a knight.

It is clear that in the time of Edward III, who ruled from 1327 to 1377, and in whose reign Chaucer grew up and wrote his earlier poems, the landed gentry were acquiring as Knights of the Shire (356)—that is, representatives of their counties—together with the burgesses who represented the towns, a preponderating place in parliament. And in local government they were increasingly important as J.P.'s. The Franklin has presided over sessions (355) of such magistrates who were appointed by royal commission. Chaucer himself was, for a time, a J.P. and an M.P. for Kent.

As Sheriff (359) of the County the Franklin was an officer preserving the King's peace and executing legal judgments, arranging for the election of M.P.'s, and so on. As a *countour* (359) he was probably an auditor and collector of local taxes like many actual men whom we know also to have been J.P.'s and M.P.'s.

He is, roughly speaking, the popular idea of a country gentleman. Never mind what claims the Knight or Monk may have to precedence or lordly virtues, it is the Franklin's solid estate and the fact that he is consequently a great householder and administrator (355) which makes him really significant.

At the same time in such unstinting hospitality the Franklin practises the virtue of *fredom*, or liberality, like the best of medieval gentlemen (*cf.* 340). That attention to food was a common trait of franklins is perhaps suggested by the fact that John Russell (mentioned above) in his *Book of Nurture* gives, in addition to the elaborate menus such as the Duke of Gloucester presumably enjoyed (for Russell served him), a menu for a "feast for a franklin." Though this meal is much simpler, there are no special menus for any others.

Medieval medicine specified in detail the food appropriate to each season (347–348), and the key to this is an understanding of medieval physiology:

Firstly, all matter was composed of four *elements* in which were variously combined four *qualities*: the qualities cold and dry = the element earth, cold and moist = water, hot and dry = fire, hot and moist = air.

Secondly, the human body was governed by four corresponding *humours*, or liquids: melancholy was cold and dry, phlegm cold and moist, choler hot and dry, blood hot and moist. These humours nourished the body, and if they became unhealthy, so did the body. Health also depended on a balance of power between the humours, and this admixture (the *complexioun*, l. 333, or 'weaving together') of humours, or 'tempering' of one by the other, produced a man's characteristic 'temperament.'

Temperaments were classified according to the humour dominant in them. Thus in the Franklin blood predominates, and he is of a sanguine 'complexion.' The Reeve is 'choleric' (587) (*i.e.*, in him choler predominates), and his character is quite different. In one of a sanguine temperament medieval psychologists expected to find a good digestion and liberality. As the mixture of humours would govern the facial appearance, a sanguine man would have a red face, and thus *complexioun* came to have its modern sense, which is present here along with the older sense.

Since the Franklin is hot and moist by nature, in a hot and moist season like spring he would eat more firm, dry foods, or he would become ill from an excess of blood. In describing his culinary arrangements, Chaucer lets his pen run riot, so that half the portrait is devoted to them.

334. Breakfast in the Middle Ages was a small refreshment to tide one over till dinner-time, which was about 10 a.m. The *sope in win* was a morsel of food in wine, which was then a usual beverage.

336–338. Chaucer probably got this information about Epicurus (*b.* 342 B.C.) from Boethius' *De Consolatione Philosophiæ*, in Book III, Prose 2 of which it is said that all human beings seek happiness (*felicitee*) but find it in different things, some in riches, some in honour, some, like Epicurus, in pleasure (*delit*). But by pleasure Epicurus meant life-long serenity of soul. Absence of pain and freedom from fear is what Epicurus desired. Far from teaching that one should eat and drink well, he taught temperance and simplicity of life.

340. St Julian was the patron saint of hospitality and travellers. Of noble birth, Julian killed his father and mother by mistake when they were enjoying his hospitality, and as a penance he built a hostel by a great river where he lodged poor travellers and ferried them across.

351. *Wo was his cook. Cf.* 'woe is me,' a relic of an O.E. construction where *woe* is a noun and *me* is in the dative case.

352. Piquant sauces were a common feature of medieval menus because the meat tended to be high.

353. *table dormant*, a fixed table. The normal dining-table was a couple of trestles and a board which were set up for the meal and taken away afterwards. The *tab e dormant* connotes a sort of running buffet.

360. *vavasour* and *franklin* often seem interchangeable terms, neither of common use, and both apparently used of a general social condition rather than a particular rank.

361. THE FIVE TOWNSMEN are members of a parish guild (*fraternitee*, 364). These benevolent religious societies multiplied throughout the fourteenth century, especially in London. Their first purpose was the financing and dignifying of burial rites for dead members (cf. *solempne*, 364: see l. 209),

and the provision of masses for their souls (hence their dissolution at the Reformation). The whole brotherhood was bound to attend funerals, dressed in uniform (363) which united all the members and made the rite more ceremonious.

In addition a parish guild often served other purposes. Quarrels between its members were to be resolved if possible within the brotherhood and not taken to court. Members who were sick or old might receive financial help, and visits were to be made to those members who might be unjustly imprisoned. Relief would be given to those impoverished by robbery or fire.

There was a second type of guild, a 'craft' guild, in which the various traders, Haberdashers, Carpenters, and so on, were severally organized. These existed for business, rather than religious and charitable purposes. Chaucer is not, of course, referring to such a guild here because five different trades would never be represented in one of them.

The dignity of Alderman referred to in ll. 369–373 is probably that of a municipal magistrate and not of a leader of a guild. The municipal government of London in the fourteenth century was drawn increasingly from the chief men of the guilds. In many towns the guildhall (370), or meeting place for a guild, was also the town hall, or meeting place for the Corporation. In the Common Council of the City of London, the Aldermen and the Mayor sat on the dais (370), or raised portion of the floor at one end of the hall, the Councillors in the body of the hall. The law required a man to have a certain amount of wealth before he could be an Alderman (373 and cf. their silver knives, 366–367). The precedence (377) which their wives would enjoy would probably be at celebrations on the vigil or eve of a great religious festival or perhaps that of a guild festival—cf. Speght's edn. *Canterbury Tales* (1598): "It was the custom in times past upon festival eves, called vigils, for parishioners to meet in their churchhouses. . . . Hither came the wives in comely manner; and they which were of the better sort had their mantles carried with them, as well for show, as to keep them from cold at the table." These women, like the Prioress, delight in dignity and reverence: by birth they are ordinary townsfolk of little pretensions.

366–368. The syntax is uncertain. L. 367 may float between the other two, Chaucer completing his comment on the knives at the same time as he begins one on the girdles because the tone and the impression intended are the same. In this case, *chaped* is understood in the second comment, though not with its exact sense of 'tipped,' probably, but rather with a general sense of 'ornamented.' But *wroght ful clene and weel* may begin a new comment quite independent of the earlier one, and it may be necessary only to understand the verb 'to be,' thus, 'Their girdles and their pouches were made well.'

379. THE COOK is called Hogge or Roger of Ware as we learn from the Prologue to his Tale (A 4336 and 4345). The Host, accepting his offer of a tale, pulls his leg, saying that he has sold in his cook-shop much food that has twice gone cold and been warmed up the next day (A 4347–4348) (*i.e.*, he is the owner of a public eating-house).

Later in the Tales (H 1 ff.) he is drunk and falls from his horse in a stupor. His *mormal* (386), which is probably *malum mortuum*, was probably caused by unclean living and especially by strong drink. The symptoms of the disease were large pustules variously described by the physicians as brownish, leaden, or black, having scabs or scales—especially unsightly in a cook. He is a connoisseur in ale, and so familiar with the taste of London ale, which seems to have been of specially good quality, that he can always recognize it.

388. THE SHIPMAN. If Chaucer intended part of the entertainment in this description to come from sly personal allusions, as is perhaps suggested by ll. 389 and 410, then we miss much, for the Shipman has never been satisfactorily identified with any actual person. Unless there are such covert allusions, the description is quite straightforward and direct.

The *barge* (410) of which the sailor is master was probably, like most ships before the fifteenth century, very wide in proportion to its length, and so almost bowl-shaped, very buoyant, but pitching viciously, and with a raised 'castle' or poop at the stern. There was probably one mast from which bellied one large sail. There would be few comforts for seamen or merchants travelling with the cargo, because cabins were by no means general, and the cargo itself was probably stacked on the ship's bottom without any more protection than a tent. Though a crude form of the compass was being used in navigation by Chaucer's time, it is not mentioned, and the indications given of the sailor's skill as a mariner suggest that he sailed chiefly round the coasts.

396–397. Casks of wine were gauged before and after carriage by sea and thus any theft could be detected. But since the merchant had travelled with the wine any deficiency at the landing end would presumably be held by any buyer as the merchant's responsibility, because he should have watched over the wine more closely. It may be that the sailor drew from the one cask that was ready tapped to provide a ration of wine for the crew on special feast-days as an act of courtesy on the part of the merchant, a provision to which reference is made in the sea-laws of the time.

404. *Cartage* is probably 'Carthage,' on the Mediterranean coast of Africa; but 'Cartagena,' in S.E. Spain, is not impossible.

408. *Gootland* is probably 'Gotland,' the island off the S.E. coast of Sweden in the Baltic Sea. Wisby, its capital, was a very important trading town.

411. THE DOCTOR. To have become a Doctor of Medicine this character must have been at university for many years, at least twice as long as the modern general practitioner. The clue to his medical skill was his grounding in astronomy (414). (See Appendix III.) The Physician believed that the stars were the cause of disease, and only when the stars were favourably disposed could it be cured, the position of the moon being of paramount importance (*cf.* 415–416). To determine the best times (*houres*, 416) for administering medicines, the Physician would probably consider the position of the important stars at the onset of the illness, and at the patient's birth (*cf.* A 1087–1090). The vital elements in

the relative positions of the stars were the 'ascendant' planet and sign. The sign and its 'lord' could be 'fortunate,' or it could be 'infortunate,' as it was when a maleficent planet, Saturn (A 2453 ff.) or Mars (A 1967 ff.) was in the ascending sign, or when such a maleficent planet had an unfavourable 'aspect' to the ascending planet. There were many other such combinations to be considered, and to *fortunen the ascendent* (417) was to 'choose a fortunate ascendant' for the treatment concerned, that is, a time when the right sign and star were just appearing over the horizon, and there were no other stars unfavourably disposed to them in the sky.

The *images* (418) he made at these suitable times were probably small objects of metal or precious stone, supposed to be imbued with the powers of the planet and sign in the ascendant at the time of their making. To procure love, for example, a talisman was made when Venus was in the ascendant. The symbol of the ascendant sign would be engraved on it, together with charms and other supposedly potent formulæ.

The planets and signs of the zodiac all had 'qualities' like the elements and humours (see THE FRANKLIN); thus in the *Astrolabe* Chaucer says, "When an hot planet cometh into an hot sign, then increaseth his heat; and if a planet be cold, then [diminishes] his coldness because of the hot sign." A four-teenth-century physician, John of Burgundy, wrote about these qualities of the stars as the causes of illness in a treatise on the Plague mentioned in l. 442: "They that have not drunken of that sweet drink of Astronomy may put to these pestilential sores [those caused by the Plague] no perfect remedy, for because that they know not the cause and quality of the sickness, they may not heal it." As the quality of the stars causing the illness was also the quality of the illness it-self, l. 420 may refer either to the *cause*, *viz.*, the stars, or to the *maladye*.

Besides these first, astronomical, causes, there were secondary causes to be considered within the patient. This is where *physic and surgerye* (413) come into play. The Doctor knows what part of the body is responsible, and what humour is diseased or in excess (421). Thus, in the Nun's Priest's Tale, Pertelote, the wife of the cockerel who suffers bad dreams, diagnoses his trouble to be an excess of 'choler,' a 'hot' humour, and says he will be in particular danger when the sun gets higher in the sky and more powerful, because since it is a 'hot' planet it will turn the excess of a 'hot' humour into an ague or fever (B 4141–4150); to correct his 'hot' condition, he must purge himself of excess 'choler.' The Doctor's drugs (425–426) would be designed, like those of Pertelote, to restore the balance of the humours and to expel any that were diseased.

There were medicines made from precious stones and metals—concocted on the principle that what is valuable in one sphere must be so in another. To discover a method of making *aurum potabile*, or drinkable gold, the most valuable of all metals, was one of the pursuits of medieval alchemists. The wit of ll. 443–444 turns on this use of gold as a heart-medicine, and on the perennial interest in the gold that lines the pocket.

The comment that this Doctor does not much read the Bible (438) reflects the far from uncommon suspicion that medicine and especially surgery were irreligious. This was partly due to their connexion with the infidel Arabs, who had contributed so much to them (*cf.* the list of authorities the Doctor knew). Moreover, medieval medicine was at least half magical (416). In the *Astrolabe*, Chaucer himself describes the theories of planets and signs in the ascendant, fortunate and infortunate, and the calculation from them of the right time to do anything and of a person's destiny, as "obser-vances of judicial matter and *rites of pagans*, in which my spirit hath no faith." Elsewhere in the *Astrolabe* he teaches that the planets do influence parts of the body, but his disavowal of 'judicial' astrology makes it possible that ll. 412–414 are intended ironically. And there were many shades of opinion about the reality and importance of astrological medicine among both medieval physicians and philosophers, especially about the usefulness of 'images' and choosing special 'hours,' so that ll. 412–414 are not an unquestioned medieval commonplace.

The intrusion of l. 438 between mention of his diet and of his clothes may seem odd. Though Chaucer's mind frequently makes such casual leaps, here it is likely that he went from lines about the temperate and nourishing food liked by the Physician to a line about the spareness of his spiritual diet through such a text as John iv, 34, "My meat is to do the will of him that sent me," or Matthew iv, 4, "Man shall not live by bread alone, but by every word that proceedeth out of the mouth of God." (*Cf.* D 1844–1845.) Though the Physician ate no excess, yet *all the same* he did not nourish his spirit on the Bible.

429–434. The Physician knows all the 'modern' medical authorities. The doctors Chaucer lists—they would probably be no more than names to most of his readers—fall into three chief groups:

1. The ancient Greek authorities, especially Hippocrates, Dioscorides, and Galenus.
2. The Arabian authorities, especially Haly, Rhazes, Avicenna, and Averroes.
3. The modern Europeans, Bernard Gordon, John Gaddesden, and Gilbert the Englishman.

Such a classification fetches out the history of medicine and much of the science of the Middle Ages, for from the great Greeks natural philosophy passed to the Arabs, the neighbours of the Greek-speaking people of the east Mediterranean, and then, with its new developments, from Arabic into the Latin of learned medieval Europe when the Arabs entered Spain from N. Africa, and when they traded with France and Italy.

The name of Hippocrates (*Ypocras*), famous as the ideal physician, is commemorated in the 'Hippocratic oath' of medical men; Greek, *b.c.* 460 B.C.

Rufus of Ephesus (430), (?) early second century A.D., a

commentator on the works of Hippocrates and author of an anatomy text-book.

Dioscorides (*Deiscorides*), (?) first century A.D., wrote what was the standard work on Materia Medica for many centuries.

Galen (*Galyen*) (A.D. 129?–199) practised in Greece and Rome, where he attended the Emperor Marcus Aurelius; wrote on every aspect of medicine, showed excellence in teaching, diagnosis, and research.

Aesculapius (*Esculapius*) was not a doctor at all but the god of medicine in the ancient world.

Rasis or Rhazes (*Razis*), a Persian (*c.* 850? 860?–*c.* 924), practised in Bagdad and was something of a philosopher and alchemist, too. His encyclopædia of medicine, like those of his successors, was a mixture of extracts from many authorities, especially the Greeks, and of original case-histories and experiments.

By *Haly* Chaucer probably means Hali ibn el Abbas, a Persian, late tenth century, whose encyclopædia of medicine, known in Latin as the *Liber Regius*, was standard until superseded by the *Canon* of Avicenna.

Avicenna (*Avicen*) or Ibn Sina (980–1037), Persian, a philosopher and generally learned man. His *Canon of Medicine* was the text-book of European medical schools throughout the Middle Ages.

Averroes (*Averrois*), or Ibn Rushd (1126–98), lived chiefly in Andalusia, that part of Spain then occupied by the Arabs, was less famous as a physician than as a commentator on the philosophical works of Aristotle.

Damascien is probably John of Damascus, *Johannes Damascenus*, under which name went a Christian Arab called Mesue the Elder (*c.* 777–*c.* 857), who practised in Bagdad.

Serapion is probably an Arab of the eleventh or twelfth century who wrote about Materia Medica in his *De Simplicibus*.

It was by the work of such men as Constantine the African (*Constantin*) that Arabic medicine was imported into Europe, for he translated Arabic into Latin. Born *c.* 1015 in N. Africa, he was educated among the Arabs, but fled to Italy and died (1087) as a monk at Monte Cassino.

Gilbert the Englishman (*Gilbertin*) wrote, probably in the thirteenth century, the *Compendium Medicinæ*, another general text-book.

Bernard Gordon (434) taught medicine in the University of Montpellier in S. France, early fourteenth century, and wrote the usual well-arranged compendium, the *Lilium Medicinæ*.

John of Gaddesden (*Gatesden*) (1280?–1361), a member of Merton College, Oxford, wrote the *Rosa Medicinæ*, another general text-book.

442. Specially profitable times for doctors were the years when Plague afflicted the country, *viz.*, 1348, 1349, 1362, 1369, and 1376.

445. THE WIFE OF BATH. Elsewhere she is simply called the *Wife of Bath*, so that *biside Bathe* (445) is hardly likely to mean a separate village near by, but rather the suburb of "St Michael's juxta Bathon," "St Michael's beside Bath," just outside the north gate of the city. *Good wif* perhaps has the sense of 'mistress (of a household),' as in Scots.

The Flemish, in whose country lay Ypres and Ghent (448), were the great continental weavers, and many of them were induced under Edward III to settle in England to foster the craft here.

Her deafness (446) is explained in the Prologue to her Tale (D 628 ff.). There also we learn much else about herself and her five husbands (460) in a garrulous confession of her need not only for marriage but also for power in the home. It was against her attempts to dominate him that her fifth husband, Jankyn, a learned man, was one evening reading aloud to her from a book insulting to women. In her anger she suddenly tore three pages out of the book and hit him.

> And he up stirte as dooth a wood leoun
> And with his fist he smoot me on the heed
> That in the floor I lay as I were deed. (D 794–796.)

And from this blow she became deaf (D 636). But Jankyn was so frightened by her lying so still that he swore there and then never again to try to master her.

Broad at the hips (472) and fenced about with a foot-cloth to keep her warm, a sharp pair of spurs ready at her heels (473), on her head an enormous hat with a brim as broad as a soldier's shield (470–471), her hose scarlet, and her face too (456–458), she might well intimidate anyone.

In her Prologue she says that she loved going visiting in order to chatter to her neighbours (D 638–640); and she has been on many pilgrimages, which she has doubtless used as excuses for seeking new sensations in the excitement of travel and showing off her gay clothes (D 559).

She is proud, and unlike the Ploughman (532) does not live charitably with her neighbours when she is not given precedence by them (449–450). When taking her offering at mass in person to the Sanctuary, as was then the custom, those of high degree going first, she will acknowledge no superior among women of her kind.

453–455. 'Her head-veils were of very fine texture.' Veils were worn in several ways, for example, over the hair and held in position by a 'caul' or net, or over a wimple, either hanging free or held by a circlet above the forehead. 'Ten pounds' is hardly meant as a serious estimate.

460. It was the custom in medieval England to solemnize marriage outside the church door. Then the couple entered the church to offer a nuptial mass.

461. 'Besides other lovers when she was young.'

463–466. Jerusalem, Rome, Galicia, Cologne (see Introduction). *Boloigne* is probably Boulogne-sur-mer in France where there is an image of the Blessed Virgin.

467. *by the weye* means simply 'on the way.' But *wandringe* implies aimless journeying, not consonant with a pilgrimage.

468. 'Gap-toothed,' having the teeth set wide apart. (*Gat* is allied to the modern English 'gate.') This is sometimes mentioned as presaging travel; but the wife calls herself *gat-toothed* (D 603) immediately before confessing that Venus

dominates her, which suggests that it may also have con-
noted amorousness.

470–471. Such broad-brimmed hats for ladies were in fashion for
country wear from the mid-fourteenth century. They were
tied on under the chin, and a veil was generally worn over the
hair beneath the hat.

475–476. *remedies of love* probably refers to the *Remedia Amoris*
of Ovid whom the medieval love poets continually cited as
their authority. This book teaches how to persuade or trick
oneself *out* of love. Ovid also wrote a work with the opposite
intention called the *Ars Amatoria,* and *art* in l. 476 reflects
this usage.

What Chaucer means is perhaps illuminated by the
Physician's Tale (C 77–82) where the old governesses of
young girls are bidden remember they have the job,

> Outher for ye han kept youre honestee,
> Or elles ye han falle in freletee,
> And knowen wel ynough the olde daunce,
> And han forsaken fully swich meschaunce
> For everemo; therefore, for Cristes sake,
> To teche hem vertu looke that ye ne slake.

Chaucer implies that you might expect the Wife in her middle
age and with such experience of love to be like these gover-
nesses, now immune to it and instructing others against it,
warning them of the sorrows and sins it involves. But he also
implies that this is just the very opposite of what she is. She
has no desire to argue anyone out of loving. It is her greatest
joy: "Alas! alas!" she says in her Prologue (D 614), "that
ever love was sin!" That is why he says quizzically "she
knew *perchaunce.*"

478. THE PARSON (*persoun*) was the rector, or receiver of the
Great Tithe of the parish. It was one of the common abuses
of the day that rectors left their parish in the care of a 'vicar,'
a substitute-priest, to whom some small portion of the rector's
tithe was paid, and went off to London where life was easier
and a *chauntrye for soules* (510) might be secured (*i.e.,* an
endowment for saying daily prayers for the repose of some

departed souls). Such a priest won a steady and regulated income and often had the rest of the day after his mass to himself. Guilds (511: *bretherhed*) maintained chapels in local churches, and to become the chaplain of one of them would also be profitable.

A special reason for this desertion of parishes was that these had become very poor through the devastation of successive plagues, so that many incumbents were scarcely prosperous. But knowing how poor his parishioners are, and how serious his punishing action would be, this priest hates to excommunicate those who committed the mortal sin of not paying their tithes (*i.e.*, that one-tenth of their income due to the church) (486). Instead he would give to them from what had been voluntarily offered to him by others, *his offring* (489), and from his own property, *his substaunce*.

Whereas in describing the Merchant, Serjeant at Law, and Friar, Chaucer enjoys their appetite for money, here he hits straight and clean at such greed in the clergy. He simply and seriously accepts this virtuous man as he did the Knight, and the implication is that those priests who are not like this one are wrong.

The Host calls him a *Lollere* (*i.e.*, a follower of John Wiclif (B 1173 and 1177)), when the priest rebukes him for swearing; and it is true that the Host says he fears he will preach at them, while another character fears he will disturb their faith. But his Tale itself is perfectly orthodox, while the work of other poets of Chaucer's time and the censures of bishops show that the ideal here presented was well-nigh a 'conventional' one. It is the serious and uncompromising piety of the Parish Priest, and his being in no way afraid to *snibben* a sinner *sharply*, that makes the Host think of the reforming zeal of the Lollards, and abuse the orthodox priest by unjustly firing their name at his head. It is as if we condemned a man as a Communist simply because he criticized conditions that Communists criticize. Though the portrait emphasizes some of the virtues Wiclif taught, it does not mention any of his distinctive doctrines. And, indeed, since

Wiclif condemned pilgrimages, the Parish Priest, if a Lollard, would not have been among Chaucer's pilgrims at all!

Chaucer remarks that this priest is a *clerk* (480: see THE CLERK). Very few parish priests of his day would have any systematic theology or ethics, for if they had been to the University at all they would in all probability have left it before graduating even in Arts, let alone Theology. Some parish priests did not even understand Latin, and thus cannot have understood their daily mass or their breviary.

496–506. The Parish Priest's illustrations are not novel. That *out of the gospel* is from Matthew v, 19. Chaucer was by no means the first poet to use it, but the neatly antithetic and balanced line he makes of it is quite a common feature of his style.

503. 'if a priest were to take heed' (to the state of being sinful while his flock is virtuous).

507. A difficulty. Perhaps a reference to the custom of selling one benefice—for the ready money—and buying a poorer one.

514. *Cf.* John x, 12 (R.V.). "He that is a hireling [*mercenarius* in Vulgate], and not a shepherd, whose own the sheep are not, beholdeth the wolf coming, and leaveth the sheep, and fleeth."

529. THE PLOUGHMAN is not one of the poorest peasantry for he appears to be in some things, at least, his own master, and when he can, will help with his free labour those worse off than himself (536–538). Since he pays tithes (539) the Ploughman presumably has some land of his own, and he probably holds it on condition of doing some labour service for his landlord (*e.g.*, carrying his landlord's dung and tilling his lands).

The portrait may be idealized. Many peasants were by no means so content with their lot. Those who had revolted and marched on London in 1381 were scarcely 'living in peace and charity' (532). The portrait bears striking resemblances to the self-description of Piers Plowman when he first appears in Langland's poem of that name, and Piers likewise thinks of going on pilgrimage. The honest peasant was traditionally the type of the sincere man, untempted by riches, humble, industrious, and devoted to the most necessary of all secular occupations, winning our daily bread. Chaucer may be preaching what peasants should be, perhaps gratifying his upper-class audience, perhaps projecting an earnest desire; but it is possible that he is portraying the traditional figure again simply for the pleasure of it, just as a more modern author might have portrayed a 'jolly Jack Tar' for the fun of it and not as a lesson to all sailors.

545. THE MILLER. Proverbially dishonest (labelled *Robin* in The Ellesmere MS. opposite his tale), the typical medieval miller enjoyed a profitable monopoly within his lord's estate since all tenants were compelled to have their corn ground at the common mill. It was hard for a customer to keep check on what was happening to his corn as it went through the mill, or to calculate exactly how much flour should be milled from the corn brought in, so that the Miller had a good margin within which he might not even be suspected. In these circumstances it was easy to take more by way of charge for milling than he ought, even if charging three times over is an exaggeration.

The reference in l. 563 is to a proverb, 'An honest miller has a golden thumb,' used to indicate that there were no honest millers. Chaucer plays on this proverb and probably means, 'As the miller was dishonest, therefore he had no golden thumb in the proverbial sense of the phrase, but nevertheless he had plenty of gold,' (*i.e.*, made much money by his dishonesty).

561. *that. I.e.*, his talking and joking.

567. A MAUNCIPLE was a purchaser of provisions in a large institution, probably under the direction of a cook or steward. Chaucer tells us that the Maunciple was unbeatably cunning in all matters of housekeeping, buying or selling; and he is slyly ironical about lawyers, since, he says, even they were not a match for his craftiness. About the Maunciple himself we learn nothing more, except that the institution he

served was a *Temple* (567). There are two 'Temples' in the Strand in London, the Inner and the Middle Temple, and they are societies of lawyers (577) named after the buildings they occupy, originally called 'the Temple' because they belonged to the Knights Templar. The Knights took their name from the Temple in Jerusalem, for their original function had been the guarding of pilgrims to the Holy Places. Their order was suppressed in 1312, and eventually the London buildings were occupied by these legal colleges which then studied Law, Latin, French, and History, and whose members, as Chaucer says, often found jobs as the managers of large estates (579) and did not simply practise law.

(The variety of Chaucer's characters is clear if we compare this portrait with the four preceding it.)

570. *took by taille*, 'bought on credit.' A 'tally' was a piece of wood like a piece of firewood, and on it a record of transactions was made in notches. These were cut across the face of the stick from side to side one under the other down its length. The stick was then split lengthwise through all the notches, and one half was given to the creditor and one to the debtor. Thus neither could cheat because on the day of settlement both halves should 'tally' exactly when rejoined.

587. THE REEVE. Chaucer specifies his 'complexion,' as he did that of the Franklin, and it is choleric (587) (*i.e.*, the humour 'choler' predominates in his disposition, causing him to be, among other things, lean and sharp-witted). (See THE FRANKLIN.)

A reeve was a manor official: but the status and work of a reeve appears to have varied from manor to manor throughout the country. He was commonly a local serf, usually one of the more prosperous; was variously chosen, perhaps by election of the rest of the serfs, perhaps by the lord's command; and served for varying periods from a year upward (601). He was the chief of the peasants on the manor for his term of office, and every aspect of its economy concerned him.

Sometimes there was a hierarchy of estate officials, the steward (579) being the immediate representative of the lord of the estate, and administering all his manors; the bailiff, perhaps, being responsible to him for a group of these or perhaps one alone, and distinguished from the reeve, who might come next and who administered one manor, in that he was appointed from outside and was not necessarily a local man. But Chaucer's Reeve, like many others on record, is probably superior to the bailiff of his manor who is mentioned in the same breath as herdsmen (603), though this may simply be indicative of the contempt felt by a junior, supremely competent and confident, for one who was actually superior.

It was often the reeve who presented the manorial accounts at the annual audit about Michaelmas to the officials appointed by the lord (594). He was responsible for collecting the lord's dues, and his was the debt if they were not paid. No one, however, by failing to pay what he owed his lord through this Reeve could cause him to be in arrears when he presented his accounts (602). He knew his subordinates too well and was too clever for them.

The inquest into the Reeve's administration would be exacting, and the minutest details of everyday country transactions are to be found recorded in such accounts still extant. Even so there can be no doubt that many an actual lord suffered from the cunning of his own reeve, and complaints against the whole kind are common. Thus ll. 593–594 may imply, 'He was very good at looking after his master's grain: so good indeed that he made much of it his very own which no suspecting auditor could deprive him of.'

605. *the deeth* = the Plague (see l. 442), or simply 'death.'

608. 'He knew how to get rich better than his master.'

610–612. Since we learn in l. 609 that the Reeve has been enriching himself secretly, it is likely that the Reeve lent to his lord wealth that he had now *prively* made his own though it was, before he had stolen it, his lord's.

620. *Baldeswelle*, now spelt Bawdswell, near Reepham in Norfolk.

622. Perhaps because of a quarrel between him and the Miller (who presumably led the company, see l. 566) mentioned later in the Tales, or perhaps out of unsociability, for he is a 'choleric' man.

623. THE SUMMONER. In the Middle Ages there were both secular and ecclesiastical courts of law. In the latter, the Bishop, or more usually Archdeacon, tried cases of non-payment of tithes, sacrilege, heresy, usury, adultery, and other offences against the law of the Church. It was a common practice to commute for money the penance assigned by the court.

The Summoner was a constable of such a court, primarily serving its summonses, but also acting as its informer and reporting breaches of its laws. There is some evidence of the corruption of actual summoners, and certainly Langland and other critics of the times are in their usual agreement with Chaucer's picture. The Summoner abuses his powerful position by taking bribes (649) and by encouraging the sinful to believe that money can buy off their judges too (657).

Excommunication by an ecclesiastical court was the 'greater curse' as contrasted with the 'lesser curse' of a parish priest, for example; and if after forty days the sinner had not complied with the ruling of the court, he was reported to the civil authorities who issued a writ for his arrest and imprisonment. This writ was called a *Significavit* (662) because its first words were "Significavit nobis venerabilis pater," and its purport was that the Bishop had signified to the King that the sinner remained obstinate after excommunication and was therefore to be imprisoned.

Ll. 623–633 concern the Summoner's fiery race, 634–646 his liking for strong food and drink and its effects on him, 647–665 his official duties and corruption, 666–668 his fantastic heartiness. There is nastiness in the first and third parts, the one of physical disfigurement, the other of sexual impropriety. His loathsome facial disease is *alopicia*, a form of leprosy, and it is doubtless connected with his debauchery (626–635) and his general liking for a heating diet (634). But

the comparison of this hideous face with that of a cherub
(624) sets the tone of the description, which is neither dis-
gusted nor compassionate: here and throughout the descrip-
tion Chaucer's poetic mind relishes the richness and unique-
ness of the phenomenon he is creating. The image he uses
is simply the fiercest burning face he could think of, for
cherubs are spirits perpetually on fire with love for God and
are represented in medieval paintings completely red.

The description is, however, uncommonly strident and
strong, like the Summoner's own garlic and onions. There
is something less reticent and subtle than usual in the line
explaining why he knew some Latin:

> No wonder is, he herde it al the day. (641.)

and more startling and violent in the line,

> "Purs is the ercedekenes helle!" seide he. (658.)

Something of the Summoner's own spirit has possessed
Chaucer's pen; he has abandoned himself with an artist's
enthusiasm to the creation of another human being.

But he has not lost his sense of the moral and religious
issues involved, and in ll. 659–662 he makes his own attitude
clear in simple words of an innocence, almost of a *gaucherie*,
odd beside the frequent sophistication of his irony, but by
no means unparalleled. That Chaucer is here poking fun at
the power of the keys, as some contend, is altogether un-
likely.

It is noteworthy, however, that as soon as Chaucer's affir-
mation of faith is done he returns to the same tone as before,
and this picture of a man physically and morally loathsome
ends with a delightful description of his garlanded head and
cake as great as a shield.

626. The sparrow was traditionally connected with lecherous-
ness.

638–641. Latin was the language in which the laws were written
and in which much of the business of the court was trans-
acted.

642–643. *I.e.*, 'you don't need to be the wisest man in christendom to say the name "Walter"—a mere bird like a parrot can learn to say it.' And it is parrot-fashion that the Summoner has learned to speak Latin phrases.

644-645. 'But if anyone tested him out on anything beyond these few terms then his ignorance was revealed.'

646. *Questio quid iuris,* 'The question is, what is the law on this point?'—the only lawyer's phrase he knows and he uses it on *all* occasions.

667. Just as barbers' shops are still sometimes advertised by a pole, so were taverns in the Middle Ages: but their poles projected horizontally and were limited to a length of seven feet.

669. THE PARDONER. The Catholic Church teaches that sins are forgiven by the power of God when the sinner is perfectly contrite, and when the priest pronounces absolution in the sacrament of penance, if it is worthily received. This forgiveness of his sins saves the sinner from eternal damnation in hell. But the western Church in the Middle Ages (like part of it to-day) also taught that there often remains due to sin, in God's justice, after the guilt has been so forgiven, a certain amount of punishment to be suffered either in this world or in purgatory. This punishment can be taken away by various means, by penance, prayer, fasting, and indulgences. An indulgence is a remission granted by the Pope or a Bishop of either the whole or a part of this temporal punishment, provided that the guilt of the sins to which it applies has already been forgiven in the manner mentioned above. Such remission is obtained in the application by the Church of the inexhaustible merits of Christ and His saints from a 'treasury' to which it has the key. Certain good works are necessary to secure an indulgence, and in the Middle Ages these might include the giving of money; in 1562 the Council of Trent forbade this latter practice because of its abuse.

Pardoners might be laymen or priests. They carried with them documents declaring a papal indulgence to all those who bought them. By this means the papacy raised money for various purposes, and the pardoners should have been merely its agents, and should have returned the money they collected to Rome. But very often pardoners were complete shams, and their pardons were forgeries. Thus a state of affairs already evil because of the popular belief that money without repentance could buy a way to Heaven was aggravated by downright fraud. Chaucer does not say whether the indulgences this Pardoner is hawking are forgeries or genuine. But there is no doubt of the spuriousness of his relics (694–706). To the proper reverencing of the relics of the Saints an indulgence is often attached and it is customary to give alms to the keeper of such relics.

Pardoners also preached as they went from parish to parish, and alms were given for this spiritual sustenance (712). The abuses to which their rôle was susceptible were fully exploited, and in 1390 Pope Boniface IX had to condemn just such tricks as this Pardoner uses. Chaucer is fully aware of the Pardoner's hypocrisy and presumably would not, if asked directly, approve of it; but as usual, in the main, he relishes what his shrewdness reveals. Ll. 689–691 are, however, more aggressive than usual, and the laughter is more harsh (cf. THE SUMMONER).

670. Near Charing Cross in London was a 'cell' of the convent of Our Lady of Roncesvalles. Roncesvalles is at the south end of a pass through the Pyrenees and on one of the roads to the shrine of St James of Compostella. The 'cell' in London was conspicuously connected with pardoners: in 1379 the Crown seized the property of the fraternity, and though it is true that it was the policy at that time to suppress all alien houses, there had been many scandals concerning the collection of alms by this particular house and by certain persons in its name.

672. The refrain (?) of some popular song.

685. *vernicle*, a representation of the face of Our Lord from the handkerchief of St Veronica (of which name the word is a diminutive) in St Peter's, Rome. Tradition says that as Christ was bearing His Cross to Calvary, St Veronica lent Him her handkerchief (or head veil) to wipe His brow, and

in return He left upon it the imprint of His face. The small copy, perhaps in metal, was a token of having made the pilgrimage to Rome.

692. Presumably, 'throughout the length of England.' *Berwik* is probably Berwick-on-Tweed, in the extreme north, and *Ware* perhaps the town in Hertfordshire, the first town of importance going north from London and twenty miles from it.

696–698. Probably a reference to St Peter's walking on the sea, losing faith, and sinking till Christ took hold of him (Matthew xiv, 29).

701–704. When he came on a poor parson he won him over by flattery, and gained his ignorant co-operation (*apes*: 706) in gulling the parishioners with false relics.

709. *lessoun*, a passage from the Bible or one of the Church Fathers read in the services of the Hours, for example in Matins which regularly preceded mass. A *storye* is probably to be understood as a series of readings, such again as occur in Matins, covering a story in the Bible or the life of a saint.

710–714. The congregation makes offerings during mass while certain verses called the 'offertory' are sung by the choir or said by the celebrant. The modern Roman rite orders the offertory *after* the sermon, but it would appear that though the Pardoner expects the offerings themselves after the sermon, he sings the verses before. In his Tale he gives an example, and in the Prologue to it a description, of his subtly deceptive preaching: with dignified and unhesitating sonority, leaning forward from his pulpit, driving his theme home with gestures and illustrative stories, he preaches always on the theme, 'The root of all evil is money-seeking.'

719. *Tabard* (see l. 20). There is no evidence of the existence of an hotel called the *Belle* in Chaucer's day.

726. 'Don't put it down to my ill-breeding.'

738. 'He is bound to repeat each word as carefully as the next.'

741. See Plato's *Timæus*, 29 B. But since there is no reason to think that Chaucer knew this work, he may have derived the quotation from Boethius' *De Consolatione Philosophiæ* (III.

Prose 12) or from the *Roman de la Rose* (15392 ff.), both of which he had translated.

752. Like the great estates of the Middle Ages the great households were staffed with various officers, and of these the Marshal was one of the most important and honourable. He was second only to the steward, and he assigned rooms to the household and its guests, supervised the serving of the lord's meals, seated every one according to their degree (in the hall, 752), and generally kept order. He carried a wand and needed just such personality, organizing ability, and good spirits as had the Host.

754. *Chepe* was one of the principal thoroughfares in the City of London, and London and Southwark still preserved their identity in Chaucer's day.

782. 'If you don't thoroughly enjoy yourselves, strike me dead'

786. 'we *granted*' (see note, l. 33).

791. 'to shorten our way with.'

793–794. *To Caunterburyward*: i.e., *toward Caunterbury*; *viz.*, 'on the way to Canterbury.' Thus, 'on the way home,' l. 794.

810–811. *were* is probably to be understood before *swore*, and *we* before *preyden*.

819–820. The wine may be a night-cap, but it is more likely a seal on the bargain.

826. A brook at the second milestone on the road to Canterbury.

829. *Ye* is probably also the subject of *recorde*, and *yow* a reflexive pronoun.

830. Proverbial: 'If you sing the same tune this morning as you did last night.'

832. 'As ever may I be permitted to drink.' *I.e.*, an asseveration = 'May I never touch a drop if whoever rebels . . . does not have to pay for . . .'

835, 838, 839, 841, 844–845. *draweth cut*, 'draw lots.' Each pilgrim in turn will draw a straw from a fistful held by the host, and whoever draws the prearranged one (836), which is called the 'cut,' will tell the first tale. Chaucer pretends not to know how it was the Knight drew the 'cut,' but it was only proper he should be first to narrate, for degree was deeply respected (*cf.* Chaucer's reference to it in ll. 40 and 744–745). The plural imperatives *draweth, cometh,* and *studieth* are the polite forms properly addressed by the Host to *my maister and my lord,* the Knight, and to the Lady Prioress, and the Reverend Clerk (*cf.* the practice in modern French).

841. *Ne studieth noght,* 'stop dreaming.' In the Prologue to the Clerk's Tale (E 5–8) the Host, rebuking the Clerk for his silence, hazards that it is due to his absorption in thinking out some philosophical problem regardless of his companions.

APPENDICES

I. CHAUCER'S ENGLISH

THE language in which Chaucer wrote was basically that spoken by his London fellow-citizens. This may be thought of as a blend of the dialects of the near-by East Midland and south-eastern areas, with the East Midland element dominant; and it was already acquiring the prestige and importance that was soon to make it the standard literary language throughout the country—the 'King's English.'

Comparatively few words in Chaucer are completely strange to the modern reader; in vocabulary and syntax (though not so often in idiom) the language of his day was not essentially different from that which we now speak. The main difficulty for the modern reader lies in the changes of meaning that many of Chaucer's words have undergone. Sometimes the context offers a hint of such a change. Thus, when the Prioress's *conscience* is twice (142, 150) mentioned in connexion with her feelings we realize that Chaucer is here using *conscience* to mean 'tender feeling' rather than 'sense of right and wrong.' But it is not so easy to discover that *chivalrye* (45) means not 'chivalry' in our weakened modern sense of 'courtesy,' but 'exercise of arms'; or that the knight is described as *gentil* because he was well-born (72). Sometimes the meaning that a word suggests to a modern reader is still farther removed from Chaucer's intentions.

Even very simple and familiar words and phrases often cannot be adequately rendered by their equivalent modern forms. Thus *foweles* (9) includes all kinds of birds; *but esy* (441) means 'only moderate'; *girles* (664) are 'young people of either sex.' Occasionally a word is used in the literal sense of its Latin original: e.g., *inspired* (6) (L. *inspirare*, 'to breathe into'). In a few words the resemblance between an old and modern form is misleading because the two have no connexion: e.g., *thinketh* (37), 'it seems,' is of different origin from the verb *to think*.

Changes in the meaning of other words (including such common verbs as *shall* and *will*) are indicated in the Glossary, and in general it will be worthwhile to consult the Glossary— unless the meaning is self-evident—whether a form is familiar or not.

The relation between the language that Chaucer wrote and the Old English (or 'Anglo-Saxon') spoken and written in England before the Norman Conquest can be clearly traced. The chief differences are in vocabulary and inflexion.

Vocabulary

Much of Chaucer's vocabulary, and many of the idioms and constructions he uses, had been adopted either from literary French or from the form of French spoken in England from the Norman Conquest till his own day (*cf.* note, ll. 124–125). Sometimes a French word or phrase had superseded an English one, sometimes it had blended with it: e.g., L. *sanctus*, O.E. *sanct*, O.Fr. *saint*; the adoption of the latter was at least rendered easier by the existence of the O.E. form. *By cause* is an example of an English phrase modelled on a French one (*par cause de*); and such phrases are important evidence of the fusion of the two languages—a fusion which resulted, among other things, in a rich variety of doublets (cf. *By foreward* [O.E.] *and by composicioun* [Fr.] (848)).

Chaucer was not necessarily the first to adopt or adapt the French words and phrases first recorded in English form in his writings, though his prestige doubtless often gave them wider currency than they would otherwise have enjoyed.

A few words and phrases are of Norse origin. They were introduced into the language by the Scandinavians who settled in the Danelaw and elsewhere, and sometimes ousted their English cognates. Thus *boone* (prayer) ousts O.E. *bēn*, and *they* O.E. *hie*. Among other Scandinavian adoptions are *felawe* and *fro*.

Inflexions

The complex system of Old English inflexions had become greatly simplified by Chaucer's day; the main inflexional differences between his language and that of the Authorized Version of the Bible being that in native English words a final *-e* or *-en*— which usually represents a levelling in unstressed position of Old English word-endings in *-e(n)*, *-a(n)*, *-o(n)*, *-u(m)*—still survives in Chaucer, with the grammatical value of the particular inflexion from which it was derived. Thus *goode*, pl. (74), is descended from O.E. *gōde*; *wonne*, p.p. (59), from O.E. *(ge)wunnen*; *sone*, nominative (79), from *sunu*; *doomes*, pl. (323), from *domas*; *hosen* (456) from the weak plural *hosan*.

As the inflexions—which in Old English indicated the case—disappeared their function was taken over by prepositions; but there are traces of an intermediate stage, where distinctive inflexion has gone, but a preposition was not felt to be necessary.

NOUNS. The genitive singular ending *-an* of the O.E. 'weak' noun had completely disappeared, but the corresponding 'strong' genitive ending in *-(e)s* had not yet been substituted in all such nouns. Hence *lady grace* (88), 'the favour of his lady'— O.E. *hlæfdigan*, *cf.* 'Lady-day.' Certain O.E. nouns had no distinctive flexion in the genitive singular or nominative or accusative plural. Thus in *fader soule* (781) *fader* represents O.E. gen.s. *fæder*; and O.E. plural forms *hors*, *gear*, and *þing* appear in Chaucer as *hors* (74), *yeer* (82), and *thing* (644, 736).

ADJECTIVES. In Old English a 'weak' form of the adjective was used after the definite article, the demonstrative pronoun, and sometimes after possessives. The endings of these weak adjectives survive as *-e*; e.g., *the hoote somer* (394).

In *oure aller cok* (823), *hir aller cappe* (586), *al er* represents the O.E. gen.pl. *ealra*, 'of all' (*hir* and *oure* = O.E. gen.pl. *hira*, *ure*).

Sometimes an adjective follows the French order: e.g., *service divine* (122); and the same sequence is found when neither noun nor adjective is of French origin (*eyen narwe*, 625); and even when the adjective is separated by a phrase from its noun: e.g., *a brooch of gold ful sheene* (160).

PRONOUNS. *Ye* (nominative) is still kept distinct from *yow* (accusative) as in the Authorized Version. *His* is the genitive singular form of (*h*)*it* as well as of *he*. The plural forms are:

> Nom: *they*
> Acc: *hem*
> Gen: *hir(e)*; *her*

The forms *they*, *their*, *them*, are of Norse origin, and first appear in areas of Norse influence.

Hise, pl. adj. (1) is a new formation in Middle English on the analogy of the plural forms *mine*, *þine*.

VERBS. The main differences between the forms used by Chaucer and those of the Authorized Version are:

Infinitive. The O.E. ending in *-an* sometimes survives as *-en*: e.g., *stonden* (88).

Present Indicative, . A 'contracted' third singular occurs in *bit* (187) = *biddeþ*.

Past Indicative. *highte* (616) is a relic of an old passive form; it is used with both past and present meaning.

The weak form *wered* (564) was later superseded by *wore*.

Imperative. The plural form in *-eth* (O.E. að) occurs often (e.g., *herkneth*, 788). It is sometimes used in addressing single persons: *draweth* (838), *studieth* (841)—*cf.* note, l. 835.

Past Participle. The past participle of an O.E. 'strong' verb had, besides a distinctive ending in *-en*, a prefix *ge-*: *-en* survives in Chaucer's language as *-e* or *-en*; the prefix often survives as *y*, but sometimes has disappeared entirely. Hence a great variety of forms: e.g., *holpen* (18), *come* (23), *yfalle* (25).

Verbs adopted from French took the ending of the O.E. weak past participle—in Chaucer usually written *-ed*: e.g., *perced* (2).

The Subjunctive. The subjunctive or 'conceptual' mood was still in living use in Chaucer's day, and not restricted to formal use and to a few set phrases, as in modern English. For examples, see ll. 68, 276, 486. But even in O.E. some subjunctive forms were indistinguishable from their indicative equivalents; and so in Chaucer *hadde* (O.E. *hæfde*) represents either past indicative (190) or past subjunctive (199).

Impersonal Constructions. Impersonal constructions are more common than in modern English: e.g., *him was levere* (293), *nedeth nat* (462), *looth were him* (486), *us thoughte* (785).

For illustrations of the changes in force and meaning of the verbs *can, coude, may, shal, sholde, wil (wol(e)), wolde,* see the Glossary.

Spelling and Pronunciation

The spelling conventions current in Chaucer's day were based in large measure upon the Old English spelling system, which had been on the whole phonetic—each letter had represented a distinct sound. French scribal customs had modified, without upsetting, this system; and by the fourteenth century two new methods of indicating long vowels were in general use:

(1) *e* and *o* were doubled; *ū* was represented by *ow* or *ou* (a specifically French practice).

(2) *-e* following a single consonant had come to be regarded as a mark of length.

The phonetic value of the long and short *vowel* sounds was probably as follows:

Short *a, e, i, o, u* as in French *patte,* English *pet, pit, pot, put.*
a after *w* had the same sound as in other positions. *Cf.* the rhymes at 151–152.

Long *a, i, u,* as in English *rather, ravine, rude.*

Long *e* had either the 'close' sound of the final *-e* of French past participles (e.g., *frappé* ($\bar{e}$)) or the 'open' sound of the vowel in English *fair* ($\bar{\varepsilon}$). Words that originally had the close sound are usually nowadays spelt with *ee* (e.g., *meet, green*). Words that originally had the open sound are usually nowadays spelt with *ea* (e.g., *heath, great*).

Long *o* had either the open sound of the vowel in *oar* ($\bar{o}$), or the close sound of the vowel in French *eau* (ō). Words that originally had one of these sounds are usually nowadays spelt with *oo, oa* respectively (e.g., *good, boat*).

y is merely a spelling variant of *i*.

au (in *straunge, remembraunce*, etc.) probably represents the sound (ʒ) still used in such modern words as retain this spelling (e.g., *paunch, vaunt*).

Final *-e* was generally pronounced, but not (except 'in pause,' *i.e.*, before a cæsura) before another vowel, or in certain plural pronominal forms (*hise, hire, youre, thise*).

As in Old English, all *consonants* (except initial *h-* in words of French origin) had phonetic value. Thus, initial *w-* (before *r*) and *c- k-* (before *n*) were still pronounced; and words ending in *-ight* did not rhyme with words in *-ite*. *L* was pronounced before *f, k, m* (*half, folk, palmer*). *R*, as in Modern Scots, was pronounced in all positions.

Except in these respects, the pronunciation of the equivalent modern word (allowing for the differences in accentuation noted on p. 124) is generally a safe enough guide.

II. THE METRE

The Prologue and most of the verse Tales are written in rhymed couplets, each line usually containing five stressed syllables. Chaucer was the first to use this measure in English verse, and he modelled his line, in part, on the French decasyllabic line. But French verse lacked the stress-accent that gives Chaucer's lines their characteristic rhythm; in a typical Chaucerian line the stresses fall as follows, with regular alternation between the stressed and unstressed syllables:

A knight ther was, and that a worthy man, (43)
He coude songes make and wel endite, (95)

—the final -e at the end of the line being lightly pronounced and making a 'feminine' rhyme.

The line usually opens with an unstressed syllable followed by a stressed one. But sometimes the initial unstressed syllable is omitted:

Twénty bóokes, cláld in blák ór réed, (294)

—or the order of the initial stressed and unstressed syllable is inverted:

Tálés óf bést senténce and móost sóláas, (798)

Occasionally the line opens with a three-syllabled foot:

With a thrédbare cópe, as is a póure scóler, (260)

"Cómeth néer!" quod he, "My lády Prióresse," (839)

Reading a passage aloud will show that the distinction between stressed and unstressed syllables is not always very marked. Prepositions, conjunctions, and auxiliary verbs are not usually susceptible of heavy-stress, and a line composed chiefly of such words may have only three or four clear stresses:

And thríes háddé she béen at Jérusálem. (463)

On the other hand, a stressed syllable is sometimes followed immediately by one bearing the same or almost the same stress ('secondary stress'):

A whit cote and a bléw hóod weréd he. (564)

Words of French origin usually retained the stress on the last syllable of the stem: *natúre, prisóun, senténce, soláas, contré*—so *philósóphré*, rhyming with *cófré* (297–298). But the English tendency to place the stress on the first syllable was already affecting such words, so that we also find *séntence, cóntre*.

In polysyllables of French origin the third syllable frequently seems to carry weaker stress than the first: *áventúre, pílgrimàge*. This is also true of polysyllables with the English suffixes *-inge*, *-nesse*: *héthènèssè* (49), *rékeninges* (760).

In such forms as *tales, olde, wonne, hadde, ycleped, servise*, the final *-e, -es, -ed* normally has syllabic value in Chaucer's verse (though it may not always have been preserved in ordinary speech); a rhyme like *Rome/to me* (671–672) would be possible only if *Rome* was disyllabic.   But in certain plural pronominal forms (*hise, hire, oure, youre, thise,* and sometimes *whiche, somme*) the final *-e* was regularly silent.

In such words as *hevene, owene, evere,* the *-e* preceding the *n/r* was apparently slurred (e.g., 804); but *seyen* ('to say') was often disyllabic.

i has syllabic value in *-ioun, -ience* (*con/sci/ence,* 142; *composic/i/oun,* 848), and in the endings *-ie, -ye(s)*, where it represents a Latin *-ia(s): vigilies* (377).

Elision

Final *-e* is regularly elided—except when it occurs 'in pause' —before a vowel or 'silent' *h*, e.g., *lange and wide* (93), *the ordres* (210), *levere have at his beddes heed* (293); and final *-o*, in unstressed position, elides similarly.

(But note the lack of elision in *Ne oinement . . .* (631) and elsewhere.)

Sometimes Chaucer uses an alternative form of a verbal inflexion in order to avoid this elision of *-e*: e.g., *To seken him* (510), as against *to seke* (17).

(The necessities of rhyme also force him to use such alternative forms: e.g., *hadde he be* (60), rhyming with *See,* as against *hadde he been* (61); for the same reason he occasionally uses a south-eastern dialect form instead of its more usual East Midland equivalent: e.g., *him leste* (787), rhyming with *beste, reste,* as against *him liste* (102).)

But despite all these considerations, it is not easy to find the rhythm of all Chaucer's lines, as we now have them: *e.g.,* l. 359.

III. ASTROLOGY AND ASTRONOMY

When we see the sun each day rise in the east, go up the sky to the south, and set in the west, we take it for granted that its movement is merely apparent, and that it is the earth we stand

on that is actually moving and revolving like a top once a day
while the sun stays still. But in the Middle Ages it was held that
the earth was stationary and that the sun went round it.

If we observe the stars night after night we see that, though
they do not move in relation to each other, the whole of the
heavens appears to move once a night, like the sun, from east
to west. This apparent motion is again attributable to the fact
that the earth we stand on is revolving. In the Middle Ages it
was held that all these stars were equidistant from the earth and
were fixed in a sphere which revolved about the earth at its
centre once every day.

We now know that the varying seasons of the year are due to
the movement of the earth in its annual orbit about the sun.
In the Middle Ages it was held that they were due to the move-
ment of the sun about the earth. But this movement was not the
same as the daily one already mentioned; it was a second and
annual movement. The sun, like the stars, had a sphere, and it
moved about the earth in it. A medieval schoolmaster might
have illustrated it in this way. Take a round ball in your hand,
put a ladybird on it, and set her walking in one direction. Turn
the ball round on its axis like a top in the opposite direction.
When you have turned the ball completely round once the lady-
bird will have done two things. First, she will have travelled
round with the ball, and secondly, she will have walked a small
distance in the opposite direction. The ladybird is the sun, the
ball is the sphere of the sun; the first movement of the ladybird
is the daily movement of the sun round the earth, and the second
is part of the annual movement. Suppose that after three
hundred and sixty-five revolutions of the ball the ladybird has
walked once completely round it in the opposite direction. That
is the number of days in the year, the time it takes the sun to go
once round the earth from west to east. The daily motion is, of
course, from east to west.

The sun, however, according to medieval theory, did not
make its annual journey in the reverse direction along exactly the
same line as its daily journey. It made it in an orbit inclined to
the plane of its daily journey at $23\frac{1}{2}°$:

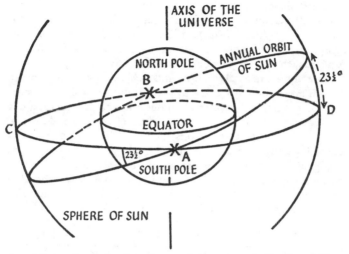

A and B are the equinoctial points, and the points A, B, C, and D are in the plane of the equator and of the daily movement of the sun about the axis of the universe.

We now know that this angle of 23½° is truly accounted for by the fact that the axis of the earth is tilted at this angle from the perpendicular as it goes through its orbit about the sun.

Suppose it is spring, and you are observing day by day that the sun rises farther east and at noon is higher in the sky. You are observing the effects of its annual 'journey.' If you imagine this annual orbit drawn on the sky and imagine the stars behind it—for they are there, and it is only the brilliance of the sun that puts them out—you will find that it is drawn approximately over twelve groups of stars, vaguely resembling certain objects and creatures like (though not including) the well-known Plough and Orion. Fill out the line of the annual orbit of the sun to a broad band either side of it to include the whole of these groups and that is the 'zodiacal circle.'

The twelve groups occupy twelve equal parts of this band, the 'Zodiac,' and each part is called a sign and is named after the constellation in it. The signs are: Aries (the Ram); Taurus (the Bull); Gemini (the Twins); Cancer (the Crab); Leo (the Lion); Virgo (the Virgin); Libra (the Scales); Scorpio (the Scorpion); Sagittarius (the Archer); Capricornus (the Goat); Aquarius (the Water-carrier); and Pisces (the Fishes).

Since there are twelve signs and twelve months in the year the sun takes about a month to get through each sign. It starts at the beginning of the first sign, the Ram, on March 12, a date equivalent to our March 21 (the difference in date is due to an error in the earlier calculations). This is the Spring Equinox, when day and night are of equal length (see A and B in preceding diagram). On this day spring begins. Since it takes a month to get through each sign it does not leave the Ram until the middle of April, and thus it spends half of each sign in one calendar month and half in the next.

RAM	BULL	TWINS
MARCH	APRIL	MAY

Most stars do not alter their positions in regard to each other, and were therefore called 'fixed' stars; but some heavenly bodies do, *viz.*, the planets, which we now know go round the sun like the earth, but which men of the Middle Ages held went round the earth like the sun. They too moved in spheres, and these were concentric about the earth and increasingly distant from it in the order Moon, Mercury, Venus, Sun, Mars, Jove, Saturn.

Like the sun, they had two motions, one daily from east to west, and one from west to east of duration varying from planet to planet. Medieval people regarded the orbits of the planets, traced on the sphere of the fixed stars, as, like that of the sun, within the belt of the Zodiac.

Two things should be remembered: first, the earth is entirely motionless in the centre, and secondly, the spheres are invisible, only the planet moving in each being seen. The system can be visualized as a Chinese puzzle where a number of boxes are contained inside each other. It is called the Ptolemaic System and was generally received until the seventeenth century when men were led to conceive of the planetary system in somewhat the same way as we do now.

It was believed in the Middle Ages that all things in this earth, and generally below the sphere of the moon, were *influenced*, though in the Christian view not *determined*, by the stars and planets. The planets, for example, had each an individual influence. Jove disposed a man to cheerfulness, sobriety, kingliness, peace, and prosperity. Thence we derive our word 'jovial.' (*Cf.* 'mercurial,' 'saturnine,' etc.) The original use of the word *influence* in English was for this 'flowing in' of astral power.

Each sign of the Zodiac had a particular 'influence,' and this was especially important when the sign was 'in the ascendant'— that is, just appearing on the eastern horizon. The influence of a sign modified the influence of any planet passing through it. Each planet had its own special 'house,' or sign, and when in it, as it circled through the Zodiac on its journey around the earth from west to east, it exercised a specially strong influence. This was even greater when the sign was in the ascendant, and the planet in it was then called the 'lord' of the ascendant.

Each planet and sign influenced a particular part of the body, as Chaucer wrote in his treatise on the 'Astrolabe' (the medieval predecessor of the sextant): "Aries hath thin heved, and Taurus thy necke and thy throte, Gemini thin armholes and thin armes."

The relations of the planets to each other in the sky (their 'constellation' or 'aspect') also modified their influence, and these relations were partly classified according to the angle subtended between them at the earth. Thus two planets were in 'opposition' when 180° apart, in 'trine' when 120° apart, in 'quartile' when 90°, 'sextile' when 60°, and in 'conjunction' when together.

Each day of the week was specially dominated by one of the planets, Sunday by the Sun, Monday by the Moon, and so on. The day from sunrise to sunset was divided into twelve parts, and so was the night from sunset to sunrise. The twenty-four hours thus determined were necessarily unequal except at the equinoxes (when day and night are equal). According to one

theory, the first hour after sunrise belonged to the planet
governing that day, and thereafter each hour in turn was

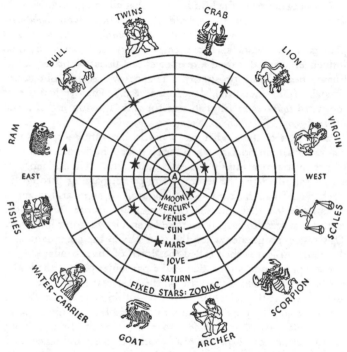

*The earth is at the centre of this diagram. Imagine yourself to be Mr A.
standing on it out of doors. Look to the eastern horizon (along the line
to 'East' in the diagram) and you see that the Ram is the ascendant
sign—i.e., just appearing above the horizon. (The arrow indicates the
direction in which you will see the heavens appear to move if you watch
long enough: the direction, that is, in which the spheres move daily.)
Venus is in the ascendant sign. Let your eyes travel directly upwards,
overhead, and then down to the western horizon. You will have passed
through the signs in the top half of the diagram. Saturn and Jove you
will have seen in 'sextile.' You will not have seen the other half of the
beavens because it is under the earth.*

assigned to the next planet in order, beginning with the most distant from the earth and working inward.

A prognostication of the destiny likely to be enjoyed by any person involved calculations about most of these factors as they stood at the moment of birth. A physician had to assess these influences when treating a disease, since the different parts of the body and the different diseases were dominated by different stars.

IV. A GUIDE TO WIDER READING

SKEAT, W. W. (editor): *The Works of Geoffrey Chaucer*, 6 vols. (Oxford University Press, 1894). Notes and glossary especially good.

ROBINSON, F. N. (editor): *The Complete Works of Geoffrey Chaucer* (Oxford University Press, 1933). Notes an excellent guide to detailed works on particular points. Glossary indifferent.

DRYDEN, J.: *Preface to the Fables* (1700).

KER, W. P.: *English Literature*: *Medieval* (Home University Library, 1912/1945).

KITTREDGE, G. L.: *Chaucer and his Poetry* (Oxford University Press, 1915/1951).

LOWES, J. L.: *Geoffrey Chaucer* (Oxford University Press, 1934/1944).

COGHILL, N.: *The Poet Chaucer* (Home University Library, 1949).

TILLYARD, E. M. W.: *The Elizabethan World Picture* (Chatto and Windus, 1943). (Medieval and Elizabethan beliefs about the structure of the universe had much in common.)

RICKERT, E. (compiler): *Chaucer's World* (Oxford University Press, 1948).

TREVELYAN, G. M.: *English Social History*, illustrated edition (Longmans, Green and Company, 1950).

BOWDEN, M.: *A Commentary on the General Prologue to the Canterbury Tales* (New York: Macmillan, 1949).

GLOSSARY

THE glossary is not intended to be a concordance but a record of such words and phrases as have changed in form or meaning since Chaucer's day. Minor changes in spelling are disregarded.

Only the first instance of a word is given. When variant spellings occur, the line reference is to whichever form occurs first.

A list of the abbreviations used will be found after the Contents.

Before using the glossary, read the Appendix on Chaucer's English and especially its warning to beware of words that look the same as modern words but have now changed their meaning. Read also the note at the beginning of the Y letter-group.

A, on (*cf.* **Amorwe**); **a Goddes name,** in God's name, 854.

Aboute, around, 158.

Aboven, above, 53.

Accorde, *pr. pl.,* accord, agree, suit, 830; *p.p.,* 818; **acorded nat (unto),** *pt. s.,* it was not suitable (for), 243–244.

Accord, agreement, agreed plan, 838.

Achaat, buying, 571.

Achatours, buyers, 568.

Acordaunt to, in keeping with, 37.

Adoun, down, 393.

Adrad, *p.p.,* afraid, 605.

Aferd, *p.p.,* afraid, 628.

Affile, *v.,* (file), make smooth, polish, 712.

After, according to, 125; to get, 136; **a. oon,** equally good, 341.

Again, again, 801.

Again, against, 66.

Al, all, 10; **alle,** *pl.,* 26; quite, entirely, 76; although, 734; **a. be,** although, 297.

Alderbest, best of all (*cf.,* **Aller**), 710.

Algate, always, 571.

Alight, *p.p.,* arrived, alighted, 722.

Alle, see **Al.**

Aller, of all, *gen. pl.* of **Al; sette hir a. cappe,** tilted the caps of them all (*i.e.,* made them look foolish), 586; **oure a. cost,** the expense of all of us, 799; **was oure a. cok,** acted as cockerel to us all (*i.e.,* woke us all up), 823.

Als(o), also, 64; as, 170, 730.

Alway, Alwey, always, 185.

Amblere, horse trained to lift two legs on same side together, 469.

Amiable, friendly, 138.

Amonges, amongst, 759.

Amorwe, on the next day, 822.

Anlaas, short, two-edged knife, broad at hilt, tapering to point, 357.

Ano(o)n, straightway, at once, 32.

Apes, fools, 706.

Apiked, *p.p.*, adorned, made trim, 365.

Areste, *v.*, stop, 827.

Arette, 2 *pr. pl.*, impute, 726.

Aright, rightly, 189; certainly, 189 (?); well, finely, 267.

Armee, armed expedition (either on sea or land), 60.

Array, dress, 'get-up,' appearance, fitting arrangement, position of matters, condition, 41.

Arrerage, arrears, 602.

Arwes, arrows, 107; **pecok a.,** see **Pecok.**

As, as if, 81; in so far as, in the way that, 390; **a. by, (in), (of),** considering, 87, 244; **a. he that,** in the manner of one who, 851.

Aspect, relative position of the planets as supposed to influence things on earth, see THE DOCTOR and Appendix III.

Assent, consent, accord, 777.

Assente, *v.*, agree (to), 374.

Assoilling, absolution, 661.

Astored, *p.p.*, stored, provided, 609.

Atte (=at the), to the, 651; **a. laste,** at last, 707; **a. beste,** see **Beste.**

Avaunce, *v.*, promote, help on, advantage, 246.

Avaunt, boast, 227.

Aventure, chance, fortune, (chance) event, accident, (trial of) chance, 25.

Avis, consideration, opinion, 786.

Ay, always, 63.

Ba(a)r(en), see **Bereth.**

Bacheler, probationer for the honour of knighthood, 80.

Bad, see **Bit.**

Baggepipe, the bagpipes, 565.

Bake, *p.p.*, baked, 343.

Balled, bald, 198.

Bargaines, bargainings, bargains, 282.

Barres, strips of metal ornamenting a belt, 329.

Batailles, battles, 61.

Bawdric, baldric, belt slung from shoulder to opposite hip, 116.

Be(en), be, 140; with verbs of motion = has, have, 77; **be,** *pr. s. subj.,* 501; *p.p.,* 56; **been,** 1 *and* 2 *pr. pl.,* 762; **beth,** *pr. pl.,* 178.

Beggestere, (female ?) beggar, 242.

Benigne, kind, gentle, meek, 483.

Berd, beard, 270.

Bereth, *pr. s.,* carries, bears, conducts (himself), acquits (himself), 796; **ba(a)r,** *pt. s.,* 105, 673, see **Burdoun; baren,** 1 *pt. pl.,* 721; **born, ybore,** *p.p.,* borne, born, conducted (self), 87.

Beste, atte and **at the b.,** in the best way, 29; **for the b.,** as intended for the best, 788.

Bet, better, 242.

Beth, see **Be(en).**

Bettre, better, 256, 648, see **Felawe.**

Bevere, made of beaver skin, 272.

Bifil, *pt. s. impers.,* (it) happened, 19; **bifalle,** *p.p.,* 795.

Bifore, Biforn, before, in front (of), in a good position, 100.

Biginne, *v.,* begin, 42; **bigan,** *pt. s.,* 44; as *pt. auxil.* = did, 827.

Bisette, *pt. s.,* employed, 279.

Bisides, him **b.,** near him, 402.

Bismotered, *p.p.,* dirtied, 76.

Bisynesse, business, diligence, care, 520.

Bit, *pr. s.,* requests, bids, 187; **bad,** 1 *pt. pl.,* 787.

Bithoght, *p.p.,* I am **b.,** I have thought, 767.

Bitwixe, between, 277.

Blak(e), black, 294.

Blankmanger, not the modern sweet made from milk, but a savoury dish of white meat (for example, chicken) cut up and heavily spiced and perhaps enriched with eggs, 387.

Blew, blue, 564.

Blisful, blessed, enjoying the bliss of heaven, 17.

Bokele(e)r, small shield, 112.

Boold, brave, big, bold, presumptuous, 458.

Boote, remedy, 424.

Boras, borax, 630.

Born, see **Bereth.**

Bracer, thick leather guard protecting archer's forearm from string of bow when released, 111.

Brawn, muscle, 546.

Breed, bread, 341; **wastel b., see Wastel.**
Breem, bream (fish), 350.
Breke, v., break, 551.
Bretful, brimful, 687.
Bridel, bridle, 169.
Brimstoon, sulphur, 629.
Bringe, v., bring, conduct, 602; *pt. s.,* 566.
Brist, breast, 131.
Britaigne, Brittany, 409.
Brode, broadly, 739.
Brood, broad, 155.
Brustles, bristles, 556.
Burdoun, the 'burden,' a technical term in part-singing; **bar to him a stif b.,** sang *or* kept up a strong bass part, 673.
Burgeis, citizen, 369.
But if, unless, 351.
By, by, through, at, in, beside, *etc.,* 25; according to, (reassured) by, 416; 244, see **As;** 467, *etc.,* see note l. 467.
Byinge, buying, 569.

Ca(a)s, chance, happening, 585; case, 655; law-cases, 323.
Cam, *pt. s.,* came, 252 c, 547.
Can, *pt. s., etc.,* recognizes, knows, knows how, is able, is skilled (in), 210; 'has,' 371; **coude,** *pt. s., etc.,* 94.
Carf, *pt. s.,* carved, slashed, cut, 100.
Carl, fellow, man, 545.
Carpe, v., talk, 474.
Catel, property, substance, wealth, 373.
Ceint, belt, 329.
Certein, particular (but unspecified), 252 b, 815; certainly, 375.
Ceruce, basic lead carbonate, 630.
Chambres, rooms, bedrooms, 28.
Champioun, prize-fighter, 239.
Chaped, *p.p.,* (the scabbard) provided with metal tip, 366.
Charge, care, responsibility, 733.
Charitable, tender-hearted, kindly, showing Christian charity, 143.
Charitee, love, 532; **out of alle c.,** full of resentment, 452.
Cheere, Chiere, behaviour, manners, demeanour, 139; look, expression of face, 728 (?); disposition, 728 (?); **greet c. made oure hoost,** our host made (us) very welcome, 747.
Cherubinnes, cherub's, 624.

Chevissaunce, business transaction, dealing for profit, borrowing at interest, 282.

Chiere, see **Cheere.**

Chiknes, chickens, 380.

Chivachye, cavalry raid, 85.

Chivalrye, feats of knightly valour, 45.

Clasped, *p.p.*, fastened, 273.

Clause, shortly in a c., in a short space of time, 715.

Cleere, clearly, brightly, 170.

Clennesse, purity, 506.

Clepen, *v.*, call, name, 643; *pr. pl.*, 620; (y)cleped, *p.p.*, 121.

Clerk, see THE CLERK OF OXFORD.

Cloistrer, one who lives in the cloister (of a convent), 259.

Cofre, chest, money-box, 298.

Colpons, shreds, bits, fragments, 679.

Com, *imp.*, come, 672.

Compaignye, companionship, company, party, 24.

Compeer, comrade, 670.

Composicioun, agreement, contract, 848.

Concubin, woman living with man without marriage, mistress, 650.

Condicioun, state, 38 (?); character, disposition, 38.

Confort, comfort, pleasure, 773

Conscience, see THE PRIORESS; 'feelings,' 398; spiced c., see Spiced.

Conseil, confidences, 665; opinion of what ought to be done, 784.

Contree, country, region, 216.

Cope, an outer garment, *probably* a cloak, 260.

Cope, top, 554.

Coppe, cup, 134.

Corage, heart, spirit, 11.

Cordial, medicine invigorating the heart, 443.

Cosin (cousin), akin to, appropriate to, 742.

Coude, see **Can.**

Countrefete, *v.*, imitate, copy, imitate with intention of deceiving, 139.

Cours, course, 8.

Courtepy, short coat, 290.

Couthe, *pt. s.*, knew (how), could, 390.

Coverchiefs, head-veils, 453.

Covine, deceitfulness, 604.

Cowthe, *p.p.*, well-known, famous, 14.

Coy, becomingly quiet, 119.

Craft, skill, art, trade, occupation, 401.

Cristen, Christian, 55.

Crois, cross, 699.

Crop, ear of corn, young shoot, 7.

Crulle, curly, 81.

Crye, *v.*, cry out, 636.

Cryke, creek, 409.

Curat, the parish priest (with a 'cure' of souls to 'care' for, and not just an assistant), 219.

Cure, care, attention, 303.

Curious, made with care, intricate, 196; skilful, 577.

Curs, curse, excommunication, 655.

Cursen, *v.*, curse, excommunicate, 486.

Cursing, excommunication, 660.

Curteis, see THE KNIGHT.

Curteisye, see THE KNIGHT.

Daunce, dance, *fig.* course of action, game, she coude . . . the olde d., she knew the rules of the game, 476.

Daunger, influence, power, **in** d., under his influence, under an obligation to him, 663.

Daungerous, haughty, 'superior,' severe, 517.

Deed, dead, 145.

Deef, deaf, 446.

Deel, (part, bit), **a greet** d., very much, 415.

Deelen, *v.*, have dealings (with), 247.

Degree, rank, 40; rank, order, 744.

Deintee, valuable, fine, 168.

Deintees, pleasurable things, 'good' things, 346.

Deis, dais, 370.

Delit, pleasure, delight, 335.

Delivere, nimble, 84.

Delve, *v.*, dig, 536.

Depe, deeply, 129.

Desdein, contempt, 789.

Despitous, contemptuous, 516.

Desport, of greet d., very entertaining, 137.

Dette, debt, 280.

Dettelees, free from debt, 582.

Devis, decision, at his d., by his decision, 816.

Digne, worthy, 141; having great opinion of one's worth, proud, disdainful, 517.

Dischevelee, with his hair hanging loose, 683.

Dispence, spending, 441.

Disport, entertainment, 775.

Docked, *p.p.*, cut short, 590.

Doomes, judgements, decisions, 323.

Do(on), *v.*, do, perform, cause, make, exert, 78; **dooth,** *pr. s.*, 98; **doon,** *pr. pl.*, 268.

Dorste, (1) *pt. s.*, dared, ventured, 227.

Doumb, dumb, 774.

Doute, out of d., without doubt, certainly, 487.

Draughte, amount drunk, 'swig,' 135; action of drawing liquor from a vessel, 396.

Drawen, *v.*, draw, attract, 519; **draweth,** *imp.*, 835; **drawe,** *p.p.* drawn (liquid from a cask), 396.

Drede, *v.*, (dread, fear), him d., *refl.* be afraid, 660.

Dresse, *v.*, prepare, 106.

Drogges, drugs, 426.

Droghte, dryness, 2; drought, 595.

Drope, drop, 131.

Drouped, *pt. pl.*, drooped, 107.

Dyere, dyer, 362.

Dyke, *v.*, make ditches, 536.

Ecclesiaste, minister, 708.

Ech, each, 39.

Echon, each one, 820.

Eek, also, 5.

Effect, in e., in fact, in reality, 319.

Elles, Ellis, else, otherwise, 375.

Embrouded, *p.p.*, embroidered, 89.

Encombred, *p.p.*, stuck fast, 508.

Encrees, increase, 275.

Ende, end, 15.

Endite, *v.*, write, compose, put into words, relate, tell of, 95 (see note); 325.

Engendred, *pt. pl.*, were produced, 421; *p.p.*, born, produced, 4.

Enoint, *p.p.*, anointed, 199.

Ensample, example, 496.

Entuned, *pt. s.*, intoned, 123.

Envined, *p.p.*, stored with wine, 342.

Er, before, 255; **er that,** before, 36.

Ercedekenes, *gen.*, Archdeacon's, 655.

Eris, *pl.*, ears, 556.

Erst, at first, before, 776.

Eschaunge, action of changing one currency for an (equivalent) amount of another, 278.

Ese, pleasure, 768.

Esed, *p.p.*, entertained, 29.

(E)sta(a)t, estate, rank, 522; state, condition, 203.

Estatlich, Estatly, stately, dignified, 140.

Esy, easy, 223; but e., only moderate, 441.

Evene, moderate ('a just mean'), proper, 83.

Everemoore, continually, 67.

Everich, every, 241; each one, 371.

Everichon, every one, 31.

Everydeel, every bit, 368.

Eye, eye, 10; eyen, *pl.*, 152.

Facultee, occupation, profession, 244.

Fader, father, 100; *gen.*, father's, 781.

Fain, gladly, 766.

Fair(e), *adj.*, beautiful, excellent, 154; desirable, 376; elegant, 'nice, 211; free from blemish, 458 (?); *ironically*, 458; a f., an excellent one, a 'beautiful' one, 165.

Faire, *adv.*, well, 'nicely,' elegantly, 94; f. and wel, in proper manner, 539.

Fairnesse, goodness of life, 519.

Falding, coarse cloth, 391.

Falle, *v.*, fall, 128; happen, 585; fil, *pt. s.*, 845; fille, *pt. subj.*, should fall, 131; (y)falle, *p.p.*, 25.

Famulier, intimate, 215.

Farsed, *p.p.*, stuffed, 233.

Faste by, very near to, 719.

Fees, fees, 317; see note, l. 319.

Felawe, good (bettre) f., (more) agreeable companion, companion (more) agreeable in wickedness, (more) companionable rascal, 395, 648, 650, 653.

Felaweshipe, companionship, company, 26.

Fer, far, 388.

Ferme, fixed sum in composition for money (obviously of varying amount) which the friar is entitled to collect, 252 b.

Ferne (1), ancient, 14.

Ferne (2), distant, foreign, 14 (?) (*pl.* of **Ferren**).

Ferre(r), farther, 48.

Ferreste, farthest, 494.

Ferther, farther, 36.

Ferthing, a fourth part, *hence* a very small portion, 134; small gift, 255.

Festne, *v.*, fasten, 195.

Fet, *p.p.*, fetched, 819.

Fetis, elegant, well-tailored, becoming, 157.

Fetisly, elegantly, with correctness, properly; nimbly, 124.

Feyne, *v.*, feign, 736; *p.p.*, 705.

Figure, figure of speech *or* rhetoric, 499.

Fil(le), see **Falle**.

Finch, innocent, naïve person, 652.

Finde, *v.*, find, provide, 648; **fo(o)nd**, *pt. s.*, 653.

Fithele, fiddle, 296.

Flaundrissh, from Flanders, 272.

Flex, flax, 676.

Flour, flower, plant, 4.

Flour de lis, *fleur de lis*, lily (either natural or heraldic), 238.

Floytinge, playing on the flute, 91.

Folk, people, 12.

Folwed, *pt. s.*, followed, 528.

Foo, foe, 63.

Fo(o)nd, see **Finde**.

For, *conj.*, because, for, since, 126.

For, *prep.*, for, 486; against, 276 (?); by reason of, 371; *with* to + *in* in order to, to, 13; **for anything**, at all costs, 276.

For(e)ward, agreement, promise, 33.

Forked, *p.p.*, divided into two points, 270.

Forme, form, in f., with decorum, 305.

Forneis, fire (under cauldron), 202; oven, cauldron, 559.

Forpined, *p.p.*, grievously tormented, 205 (?); wasted away, 205.

Forster, forester, 117.

Fortunen the ascendent, see THE DOCTOR.

Foryeve, *v.*, forgive, 743.

Fother, (cart-)load, 530.

Foul, filthy, wicked, 501.

Fowel, bird, 9.

Fram, from, 15.

Frankelein, see THE FRANKLIN.

Free, given readily *or* willingly, 852.

Freend, friend, 299.

Fressh(e), fresh, bright, pure, 90; freshly, brightly, 365.

Fro, from, 44; **f. . . ward** (*cf.* 'towards'), on the way from, 397.

Ful, fully, very, quite, 22.

Fustian, coarse material of cotton and flax, probably unbleached, 75.

Gadrede, *pt. s.,* gathered, 824.

Galingale, an aromatic root, 381.

Game, fun, entertainment, match, 853.

Gamed, thogh he g. or smerte, though he was enjoying himself or suffering, *hence* in all circumstances (for which it is one of a number of common phrases in M.E.), 534.

Gan, *pt. s.,* began, 822; as *auxil.* = did, 301.

Garleek, garlic, 634.

Gat, see Gete(n).

Geere, appliances, 'kitchen things,' 352; dress, accoutrements, equipment, tackle, 365.

Gentil (*cf.* THE KNIGHT), noble and tender-hearted, 72; worthy, 718; *used ironically,* 567.

Gerland, garland, 666.

Gerner, garner, 593.

Geten, *p.p.,* obtained, procured (for), 291; **gat,** *pt. s.,* 703.

Ginglen, *v.,* to jingle, 170.

Gipser, purse or pouch hanging from the belt, 357.

Girles, young people of either sex, 664.

Gise, at his owene g., to do what he liked with, 663.

Gobet, piece, 696.

Goliardeis, great talker, 560.

Good, property, wealth, 611; **by his propre g.,** on his own income. 581.

Goodly, kindly, readily, 803.

Goon, *v.,* go, walk, 12; 2 *pr. pl.,* 769; **g. al bifore,** go first, have precedence in going, 377.

Governaunce, conduct of business, proceedings, 281.

Governing, control, 599.

Governour, leader, director, 813.

Gowne, upper garment, 93.

Grace, mercy, favour, 88.

Graunted, 1 *pt. pl.,* consented to, agreed to, granted, 786; *p.p.,* 810.

Grece, grease, 135.

Greet, great, 84; 'great,' excellent, 203; a great (one), on a large scale, 339.

Grehoundes, greyhounds, 190.

Grene, green (colour, thing, *etc.*,), 103.

Gretter, greater, 197.

Gretteste, greatest, 120.

Greye, grey (*possibly* light blue), 152.

Gris, grey fur, 194.

Grope, *v.*, test, examine, search out, 644.

Ground, texture, 453.

Halwes, shrines of saints, saints, 14.

Han, see **Have.**

Happe, *v.*, happen, 585.

Hardily, certainly, 156.

Hardy, courageous, daring, 405.

Harlot, 'fellow,' rogue, 647.

Harlotries, buffoonery, scurrilous joking, 561.

Harneised, *p.p.*, mounted, 114.

Harre, hinge, 550.

Haunt, use, habit, practice, 447; resort, customary area, 252 c.

Have, *v.*, have, preserve, and as *auxil.*, 548; **han,** as *auxil.*, 795.

Haed, head, 198.

He(e)ld, see **Holde(n).**

He(e)ng, *pt. s.*, hung, 160; **henge,** *pt. pl.*, 677.

Heepe, (heap), crowd, host, 575.

Heer, hair, 589; **heris,** *pl.*, 555.

Heere, *v.*, hear, 169; **herde,** *pt. s.*, 221; **herd,** *p.p.* 849.

Heigh, high, 316; **in h. and lough,** in everything, 817.

Helpe(n), *v.*, help, 258; **holpen,** *p.p.*, 18.

Hem, them, 11.

Henge, see **He(e)ng.**

Hente, *v.*, catch, get, 299; *pt. s.*, 698.

Herberwe, finding a harbour, harbourage, 403; inn, 765.

Herd(e), see **Heere.**

Heris, see **Heer.**

Herkneth, *imp.*, listen, 788.

Herte, heart, seat of the 'feelings,' one's emotional nature, one's inmost being, disposition, 150.

Hertely, heartily, with all my heart, 762.

Hethenesse, parts inhabited by the heathen, 49.

Heve, *v.*, heave, lift 550.

Hevene, Heaven, 519.

Hewe, complexion, colour, 394.

Hider, hither, 672.

Hier, upper, 399.

Hierde, herdsman, 603.

Highte, *pt. s.*, was called, 616.

Him, himself, 87.

Himselven, himself, 184.

Hindreste, hindmost, 622.

Hine, servant, labourer, 603.

Hipes, hips, 472.

Hir, their, 11; of them, 586.

Hir, her, 120.

Hise, his, its, 1.

Holde(n), *v.*, hold, consider, esteem, follow; **heeld,** *pt. s.*, 176; hoold, *imp.*, 783; holden, *p.p.*, 141.

Holpen, see **Helpe(n).**

Holt, wood, 6.

Holwe, hollow, hungry, lean, 289.

Hond, hand, 399.

Honeste, respectable, creditable, of good moral character, 246.

Honour, see THE KNIGHT; (virtuous) renown, 46; dignity, 582.

Hoole, whole, 533.

Hoold, see **Holde(n).**

Hoolly, wholly, 599.

Hooly, holy, 17; **h. writ,** the Holy Scriptures, 739.

Hoom, home, 400.

Hoomly, in a homely way, 328.

Hoot(e), hot, 394; hotly, fervently, 97.

Hors, horse, 168; *pl.*, 74.

Hose, covering for feet and legs, hose; **hosen,** *pl.*, 456.

Hostelrye, inn, 23.

Hostiler, innkeeper, 241.

Hous, religious house, 252; dwelling house, 343.

How, how, 766; **h. men him calle,** what his name is, 284.

Humour, see THE FRANKLIN, 421.

Hy(e), high, 271; not shallow or trivial, 306.

Ilke, same, very, 64.

Inne, in, 41.

Inspired, *p.p.*, blown upon, breathed life into, 6.
Iren, iron, 500.

Janglere, jester, chatterbox, 560.
Japes, tricks, 705.
Jet, fashion, of the newe **j.,** in the latest style, 682.
Jolitee, fun, festivity, 680.
Juge, judge, 814.
Juggement, decision, 778.
Juste, *v.*, joust, 96.

Keepe, took k., took notice, 398; see note, l. 50.
Kepe, *v.*, keep, care, take care, guard, 130.
Kepere, head (of the community), 172.
Knarre (knotted thing), man knotted with muscle; **thicke k.,** thickset, brawny fellow, 549.
Knobbes, knobs, pimples, 633.
Knowe, *v.*, recognize, know, understand, 382; **knowen,** 2 *pr. pl.*, 642; **yknowe,** 423.

Laas, string, 392.
Lady, lady, *gen.*, lady's, 88.
Lacked, *pt. s.*, *impers.*, **him l.,** he lacked, 756.
Large, wide, broad, large, 472; freely, broadly, 734.
Lat, see **Lete.**
Late, lately, recently, 77.
Latoun, yellow metal, identical with or closely resembling brass, 699.
Lay, (1) *pt. s.*, lay, lodged, was, 20.
Lazar, leper, 242.
Leed, cauldron, 202.
Le(e)ne, lean, thin, 287.
Leet, see **Lete.**
Lefte, *pt. s.*, left (off), ceased, omitted, 492.
Leid, *p.p.*, laid, 81.
Lene, *v.*, lend, give, 611.
Lenger, longer, 330.
Leste, see **List.**
Lete, *v.*, let, leave, forsake, **leet,** *pt. s.*, 128; **lat,** *imp.*, 188; **l. se,** let us see, 831; **l. be,** let be, away with, 840.
Letuaries, electuaries, medicinal paste made of powder mixed with honey or syrup of some sort, 426.

Levere, dearer, **him was l.** (it was dearer to him), he would rather, 293.

Lewed, ignorant, 502.

Licour, liquid, moisture, 3.

Lik, like, 412.

Liketh, *pr. s. impers.*, **yow l.**, it pleases you, you like, 777.

Likned, *p.p.*, likened, 180.

Lipsed, *pt. s.*, lisped, 264.

List, pleasure, delight, 132.

List, *pr. s. impers.*, **him (me, thee, yow) l.**, it pleases him (me, *etc.*), 583; **leste**, *pr. s., subj.*, 828; **liste**, *pt. s.*, 102.

Listes, palisades enclosing tilting-ground, tilting-ground, 63.

Litarge, litharge, yellow oxide of lead, 629.

Litel, little, 87.

Lodemenage, pilotage, 403.

Lond, land, 14; country, **up on l.**, down in the country, 702.

Longen, *pr. pl.*, desire, long, 12.

Loore, teaching, 527.

Looth, **ful l. were him**, most hateful would it be to him, 486.

Lordinges, gentlemen, 761.

Lough, low, 522; 817, see **Heigh.**

Lovyere, lover, 80.

Lowe, drooping, the web of each feather lying close to its shaft, 107.

Lowely, humble, 99.

Luce, luce (fish), 350.

Lust, joy, pleasure, desire, 192.

Lusty, joyful, lively, vigorous, gay, 80.

Maad, see **Make(n).**

Magic natureel (*cf.* THE DOCTOR), art of influencing events by occult control of nature (but without invoking demons, which is *black* magic), 416.

Maister (*cf.* THE FRIAR), master, superior, 576.

Maistrye, **for the m.**, as if aiming at the mastery, *hence*, surpassing all others, extremely, 165.

Make(n), *v.*, make, compose, draw up, cause, 184, see note, l. 95; 785, see **Wis**; 1 *pr. s.*, 775; *pr. pl.*, 9, **maked**, *pt. s.*, 526, see **Spiced**; **maad**, *p.p.*, 212.

Male, bag, wallet, 694.

Maner(e), kind (of), 71; manner, 140.

Manhod, manliness, valour, 756.

Marybone, bone containing edible marrow, 380.

Mateere, matter, affair, 727.

May, *pr. s.*, is able to, has power to, may, 230.

Medlee, motley, parti-coloured (?); *perhaps* refers to way dyeing is done, *viz.* after washing the wool but before weaving it—cloth of such wool was woven in stripes, 328.

Meede, reward, 770.

Meede, meadow, 89.

Men, *impers. subject* (*cf.* Fr. *on*), one (unstressed form of **Man**), 149.

Mene, 1 *pr. s.*, mean, intend, am disposed, 793.

Mercenarye, hireling, 514.

Mere, mare, 541.

Merye, Mirye, Mury(e), merry, happy, gay, pleasant, 208.

Meschief, misfortune, trouble, 493.

Mesurable, moderate, temperate, 435.

Mete, food, meat, 136; main meal of the day, 348; at m., at table, 127.

Might, power, 538.

Mirthe, entertainment, 759.

Mirye, see **Merye**.

Miscarye, *v.*, come to harm, 513.

Mo, more (in number), 576.

Moiste, not dried up with age, glossy as new, supple, 457.

Moore, more, 219.

Moost, chiefly, mostly, 561.

Moot(e), *pr. s.*, ought to, is bound, 232; *pr. pl.*, 742; **moste**, *pt. s.*, 712; **mote**, 1 *pr. s. subj.*, may be permitted, 832.

Morne, morning (milk), 358.

Mortreux, of fish or meat. The chopped or ground flesh was seasoned variously, but heavily, and mixed with yolks of eggs and grated bread, 384.

Morwe, by the m., in the morning, 334.

Moste, Mote, see **Moot(e)**.

Motlee, cloth of mixed colour, 271.

Muche and lite, great and small, rich and poor, without any exceptions, 494.

Muchel, much, greatly, 132, 211.

Murierly, more merrily, 714.

Mury(e), see **Merye**.

Muwe, cage or coop in which birds were confined for fattening, 349.

Myster, trade, occupation, 613.

Nacions, nations, representatives of a nation, 53.

Namo, no more (in number), 101.

Namoore, no more, 98.

Narwe, small, narrow, 625.

Nas (=ne was), was not, 251.

Nat, not, 74.

Nathelees, nevertheless, 35.

Naught, nothing, 756.

Ne, not (often only intensifying negative), 70; nor, 129.

Nedeth, *pr. s.,* there is need, 462; **what n.,** what is the need of, 849.

Neer, near, nearer, 839.

Neet, cattle, 597.

Nice, scrupulous, foolish, 398.

Nightertale, by n., in the night-time, 97.

Noght, not, 107.

Nolde (=ne wolde), would not, 550.

Nombre, number, 716.

Nones, Nonis, for the n., for the particular purpose, expressly, 379 (?); specially, particularly ('I'll say,' 'believe me'), 523; (tending to a mere tag), 379 (?).

Noon, none, 318; no, 594.

Noot (=ne woot), 1 *pr. s.* know not, 24.

Norissing, nourishment, 437.

Northfolk, Norfolk, 619.

Nosethirles, nostrils, 557.

Not-heed, a head with hair cropped short, 109.

Nowthe, as n., just now, at present, 462.

Ny, nearly, closely, 588.

O, one, 304.

Of, of, 2; in, 69; as to, concerning, 83; some, 146; out of, 725.

Offertorye, see note, ll. 710–714.

Ofte, often, 55; **o. time(s), o. sithe(s),** often, 52.

Oille of tartre, oil obtained from cream of tartar, 630.

Oinement, ointment, 631.

Oinons, onions, 634.

Old, old, old-fashioned, 174.

Ones, once, 765.

Oon, one, 777; **many o.,** many a one, 317; **o. and o.,** one by one, severally, 679.

Ooth, oath, 120.

O(o)ther(e), other, 603; **o. two,** two others, 794; **oother,** the other, 427.

Opinioun, opinion, conclusion, 183.

Ordre, order, religious order, 214.

Ounces, small quantities, shreds, 677.

Outrely, utterly, absolutely, outright, plainly, 237.

Over, upper, 133.

Overal, (1) everywhere, 547; (2) beyond all, especially, 216.

Overeste, uppermost, outer, 290.

Over-spradde, *pt. s.,* covered (over), 678.

Owene, own, 213.

Owher, anywhere, 653.

Paas, walking-pace (?), 825.

Pace, *v.,* go, proceed, pass away, 175; surpass, 574; 1 *pr. s.,* 36.

Pardee (*=par dieu*), certainly, 'upon my word' (a common oath), 563.

Parfit, perfect, 72.

Parisshens, parishioners, 482.

Partrich, partridge, 349.

Patente, a royal letter *open* for all men's inspection, 315.

Pecok arwes, arrows with peacock feathers, 104.

Pees, peace, 532.

Peined hir, *pt. s. refl.,* she took pains, 139.

Perced, *p.p.,* pierced, 2.

Perchaunce, perhaps, by chance, 475.

Pers, cloth of blue-grey colour, 439.

Person(e), Persoun, see THE PARSON; person, 521.

Pestilence, plague, 442.

Piled, *p.p.* as *adj.,* scraggly, very thin, 627.

Pilwe-beer, pillow-case, 694.

Pinchen, *v.,* find fault (with), cavil (at), 326; *p.p.,* pleated, fluted, 151.

Pitaunce, allowance, gift, 224.

Pitous, pious, full of pity, tender, 143.

Plein, full, perfect, 315; fully, entirely, clearly, plainly, 327.

Pleinly, fully, openly, plainly, without embellishment, 727.

Plesaunt, pleasing, agreeable, 138.

Plesen, *v.,* please, 610.

Pleye(n), *v.,* play (on an instrument), 236; be playful, make fun, amuse (self), 758.

Point, point, 114; precise matter in discussion, aim, conclusion, end,

790; **in good p.**, (*cf.* Fr. *en bon point*), in good shape *or* condition, prosperous-looking, 200.

Pomely, marked with round spots, dappled, 616.

Poraille, poor people, 247.

Port, behaviour, bearing, 69.

Poudre marchant, a flavouring powder made from several spices and very pungent, 381.

Poure, poor, 225.

Poure, *v.*, pore, look closely, 185.

Poynaunt, pungent, piquant, 352.

Practisour, practitioner, 422.

Prelaat, prelate, ecclesiastical dignitary of high rank, 204.

Presse, curling irons *or* papers, 81; clothes press, 263 (?); cupboard, 263 (?).

Preved, *p.p.*, proved, shown to be (true), 485.

Prikasour, hard-rider, 189.

Priketh, *pr. s.*, wounds sharply, urges, stimulates, spurs, rides, darts, 11.

Priking, tracking a hare (by its 'pricks' *or* footprints), 191 (?); hard-riding, spurring (see **Priketh**), 191.

Pris, reputation, renown, worth, prize, 67; price, 815.

Prively, secretly, 609.

Profit, advantage, gain (spiritual *or* material), 249.

Propre, own, 540.

Proprely, literally, correctly, in character, 729.

Proved wel, *pt. s.*, was well seen, was very evident, 547.

Pulle, *v.*, fleece, 'take in,' 652; *p.p.* as *adj.*, plucked, 177.

Pultrye, poultry, 598.

Purchace, *v.*, acquire possessions, get rich, 608.

Purchas, gaining one's sustenance, making profit (*esp.* irregularly), acquiring property by personal action instead of inheritance, 256.

Purchasing, acquisition of property by means other than inheritance, 320.

Purchasour, an acquirer of possessions in any other way than by inheritance, 318.

Purtreye, *v.*, draw, 96.

Quik, lively, acute, 306.

Quik-silver, mercury, 629.

Quite, *pr. s. subj.*, reward, give in return, 770.

Quod, *pt. s.*, said, 788.

Rage, *v.*, act as if mad, scold, behave wantonly, 257.

Ram, have the r., win the (ram as) prize, 548.

Rather, sooner, 487.

Raughte, *pt. s.*, reached, 136.

Recchelees, undutiful, careless of conduct, 179.

Recorde, 2 *pr. pl. refl.*, remember, call to mind (*cf.* Fr. *se recorder* = 'to call to mind'), 829.

Rede, *v.*, read, 709.

Reed(e), red, 90.

Reed, counsel, adviser, 665.

Reherce, *v.*, repeat, 732.

Rein, rain, 492.

Reised, *p.p.*, gone on a military expedition, 54.

Rekene, *v.*, calculate, compute, 401.

Rekening, account, 600.

Religioun, man . . . of r., one in holy orders, 477.

Remedies, see note, ll. 475–476.

Remenaunt, rest, 724.

Renning, running, at a r., in one run, 551.

Rente (a giving back), (just) reward, (proper) return for land leased, (orthodox) income, 256.

Reportour, recounter, narrator, (assessor?), 814.

Reso(u)n, reason, decorum, 37; argument, 274; **as was r.,** as was reasonable *or* right, 847.

Reste, to r., (gone) to rest, 30.

Reuled, *p.p.*, ruled, 816.

Reverence, respect, deference, 141; condition of being respected, 312.

Ride(n), *v.*, ride, go (to war) as a knight, 27; **riden,** 2 *pr. pl.*, 780; 1 *pt. pl.*, 825; *p.p.*, 48; **rood,** *pt. s.*, 169; **to r. out,** to go on horseback on an expedition of war, 45.

Right, just, exactly, very, altogether, 257.

Rood, see Ride(n).

Roos, *pt. s.*, rose, 823.

Rooste, *v.*, roast, 383; *p.p.* as *adj.*, 147.

Roote, root, 2 (?); to the r., *fig.* to the very bottom, 2.

Rote, by r., in a mechanical manner, by heart, 327.

Rote, stringed instrument *probably* like a violin, 236.

Rouncy, heavy horse (like cart-horse) such as might be ridden by fully armed knight, 390.

Rounded, *pt. s.*, hung in a rounded form, 263.

Route, company, 622.

Royalliche, royally, like a queen, 378.
Rudeliche, roughly, unmannerly, 734.

Saide, see **Seye.**
Sangwin, blood-red, see THE FRANKLIN, 333; cloth of blood-red colour, 439.
Saucefleem, covered with pimples, 625.
Saugh, see **Se.**
Sautrye, a kind of harp, 296.
Scaled, *p.p.* as *adj.*, scabby, 627.
Scarsly, economically, frugally, 583.
Scathe, harm, 'a pity,' 446.
Science, knowledge, 316.
Sclendre, thin, 587.
Scoleye, *v.*, study, 302.
Seche, *v.*, seek, **for to s.,** to be sought for, 784.
Seege, siege, 56.
Seeke, sick, ill, 18.
Se, *v.*, see, look, 831; **saugh, seigh,** 1 *pt. s.,* 193; **saugh,** *pt. s.,* 144.
Sene, visible, apparent, 134.
Seid(e), see **Seye.**
Seigh, see **Se.**
Seil, sail, 696.
Seith, see **Seye.**
Seke(n), *v.*, seek, 13.
Selle, *v.*, sell, 278.
Semed, *pt. s.,* seemed, appeared, 313; **it s. me,** it seemed to me, 39.
Semely, Semily, fitting, suitable, 751; becomingly, fittingly, decorously, 123.
Semicope, probably a shorter **Cope,** *q.v.,* 262.
Semily, see **Semely.**
Sendal, thin, rich silk cloth, 440.
Sentence, meaning (as distinguished from the wording or the story), sense, a saying, opinion, 306.
Servisable, willing to serve, 99.
Sethe, *v.*, seethe, boil, 383.
Sette, *v.*, place, set, put, appoint, fix, 815; *pt. s.,* 507; 586, see **Aller; set,** *p.p.,* 132.
Seye, Seyn, *v.*, say, 181; **seith,** *pr. s.,* 178; **seide,** 1 *pt. s.,* 183; **saide, seide,** *pt. s.,* 70; **seid,** *p.p.,* 305.
Shadwed, *p.p.,* shaded, 607.

Shake, *p.p.*, shaken, 406.

Shal, *v. auxil.* (1) *pr. s.*, am (is) to, must, shall (be), will, 187; **sholde** *pt. s.* and *pl.*, should, would, ought to, was (were) to, 184.

Shamefastnesse, modesty, 840.

Shape(n), *v. refl.*, plan, intend, arrange, 809; 2 *pr. pl. refl.*, 772.

Shaply, in the right shape, suitable, fit, 372.

Shave, *p.p.*, shaved, 588.

Sheeldes, French coins having shield stamped on one side, 278.

Sheene, bright, beautiful, splendid, 115.

Shine, shin, 386.

Shires, shire's, 15.

Shiten, *p.p.*, defiled, dirty, 504.

Sho, shoe, **hadde noght a s.**, had not a penny, 253.

Sholde, see **Shal.**

Shoon, *pt. s.*, shone, 198.

Shorte, *v.*, shorten, 791.

Shortly, in a short time, soon, 30.

Short-sholdred, square-built, thick-set, 549.

Shoures, showers, 1.

Shuldres, shoulders, 678.

Sike, sick, 245.

Sikerly, certainly, surely, 137.

Sin, since, 601.

Sinne, sin, 561.

Slee, *v.*, slay, 661; **slain**, *p.p.*, 63.

Sleighte, cunning, 604.

Slepen, *pr. pl.*, sleep, 10.

Smal(e), small, 9; thin, high (of voice), 688.

Smerte, smartly, sharply, 149.

Smerte, him s., *pt. s. subj. impers.*, it might grieve him, 230; 534, see **Gamed.**

Smoot, *pt. s.*, struck, 149.

Smothe, smooth, 690; smooth(ly), 676.

Snewed, *pt. s.*, snowed, 345.

Snibben, *v.*, reprove, 523.

So as, as, 39.

Sobrely, serious(ly), quiet(ly), temperate(ly), 289

Solaas, entertainment, delight, 798.

Solempne, solempnely, see note, l. 209.

Somdel, somewhat, 174.

Somer, summer, 394.

Somtime, once, occasionally, 65.

Sondry, various, 14.

Sone, son, 79.

Songe, *p.p.*, sung, 266.

Sonne, sun, 7.

So(o)ng, *pt. s.*, sang, 122.

Soore, sorely, 148.

Soote, sweet, genial, pleasant, 1.

Sooth, truth, 284.

Soothly, truly, 117.

Soper, last meal of the day, 348.

Sort, destiny, fate, chance, 844.

Sothe, truth, 845; **for s.**, in truth, truly, 283.

Soun, sound, 674.

Souple, supple, 203.

Soverein, supreme, very high, 67.

Sowed, *p.p.*, sewn, 685.

Sowne, *v.*, sound, play upon, 565; **sowninge**, *prp.*, relating to, declaring (?), 275; **s. in**, having a tendency towards, a connexion with, 307.

Space, space of time, opportunity, 35; course, 176.

Spak, see **Speke(n)**.

Spare, *v.*, spare, refrain, 192.

Sparwe, sparrow, 626.

Special, **in s.**, specially, 444.

Speede, *pr. s. subj.*, may prosper, 769.

Speke(n), *v.*, speak, 462; (1) *pr. s. subj.*, 727; **spak**, *pt. s.*, 124; **to s. of**, as regards, 142.

Spere, spear, 114.

Spiced, **maked him a s. conscience**, cultivated a tough, spoilt, insensitive conscience, 526.

Spores, spurs, 473.

Springe, *v.*, dawn, 822.

Squier, see THE SQUIRE.

Staat, see **(E)sta(a)t**.

Statut, enactment of king and his council, Act of Parliament, 327.

Stelen, *v.*, steal, 562.

Stemed, *pt. pl.*, glowed, 202.

Stepe, prominent, glaring, 201.

Sterres, stars, 268.

Stif, strong, 673.

Stiwardes, stewards, see THE REEVE, 579.

Stonde(n), *v.,* stand, be, be placed, 88; **s. at,** abide by, 778.

Stoon, stone, 774.

Stoor, stock of a farm, 598.

Stot, stout horse, 615.

Stout, strong, 545.

Straunge, foreign, unfamiliar, exciting wonder, 13.

Streight, straightway, directly, 671.

Streit, strict, 174.

Streite, tight(ly), *so with* **yteyd,** close-fitting, 457.

Strem, stream, 464; *pl.,* currents, 402.

Strike, hank (of flax), 676.

Strondes, shores, 13.

Stuwe, pond or tank in which fish were kept until needed, 350.

Subtilly, craftily, cunningly, 610.

Suffisaunce, enough, contentment, 490.

Surcote, upper coat, 617.

Sweete, genial, pleasant, agreeable, fragrant, 5.

Swerd, sword, 112.

Swere, *v.,* swear, 454; **swore,** *p.p.,* 810.

Swich(e), such, 243; the previously described, 3.

Swin, swine, 598.

Swink, labour, 188.

Swinken, *v.,* labour, 186.

Swinkere, labourer, worker, 531.

Ta(a)k, see **Take.**

Tabard, upper garment of coarse cloth worn by peasants and the humble, 541.

Taffata, silk cloth, 440.

Take, *v.,* take, 34; *pr. s. subj.,* see note, l. 503; **ta(a)k,** *imp.,* 789.

Takel, arrows, equipment, 106.

Tale, tale, account, 330.

Talen, tell tales, converse, 772.

Tapicer, upholsterer, 362.

Tappestere, (female?) tapster, 241.

Targe, light shield, 471.

Taryinge, delay, 821.

Teche(n), *v.,* teach, instruct, 308.

Telle(n), *v.,* tell, give (account), 38; **tel,** *imp.,* 808.

Termes, terms, 639; **in t.,** in express words, in set expressions, 323.

Text, saying, 177.

Thank, expression of gratitude, **have a t.**, be thanked, 612.

Than(ne), then, 12.

That, *conj.*, that (as a consequence), so that, 32; often subjoined to other *conjs.*, *e.g.*, if (144), and to *advs.*, *e.g.*, whan (1).

That, *rel.*, *pron.*, who, which, that, that which, 10; **that oother**, the other, 113; **that ... his**, whose, 604.

Ther, there, 43; where, 547; in that business, in those circumstances, 259.

Theras, in that place where, where, 172; to that place which, 34.

Therto, in addition, moreover, 48.

Therwithal, with it, by means of it, 566.

Thicke, see **Knarre**.

Thilke (=the ilke), that same, such a, 182.

Thing, thing, matter, affair, 175; composition, work of art, story, legal document, 325; 276, see **For**; *pl.*, 644, *etc.*

Thinke (1), *v.*, think (of), 346. (O.E. thenc(e)an. In M.E. this verb was confused with **Thinke** (2).)

Thinke (2), *v. impers.*, seem; **me thinketh it**, it seems to me, 37; **it thoughte me**, it seemed to me, 385; **him (us) t.**, it seemed to him (us), 682. (O.E. **thync(e)an**. In M.E. this verb was confused with **Thinke** (1).)

Thinne, thin, scanty, 679.

Thise, these, 701.

Tho, those, 498.

Thombe, thumb, 563.

Thoughte, see **Thinke** (2).

Thries, thrice, 63.

Thriftily, successfully, prudently (?), handily (?), 105.

Til, to, 180.

Toft, tuft, 555.

Togidre, together, 824.

Tollen, *v.*, take toll, make charge, 562.

Tope, top (of head), 590.

Toun, (country) parish, 478.

Tretis, slender, graceful, 152.

Trewe, true, honest, faithful, 531.

Trewely, truly, 761.

Trompe, trumpet, 674.

Trouthe, see THE KNIGHT; **by my t.**, by my pledged word, 'believe me,' 763.

Trowe, 1 *pr. s.*, think, believe, ='take my word for it,' 155.

Trussed, *p.p.*, packed, 681.

Tucked, *p.p.*, tucked, having a girdle about his waist 'tucking up' his coat, 621.

Tweye, two, 704.

Twinne, 1 *pr. pl.*, go, depart, 835.

Undergrowe, *p.p.*, of slight build, 156.

Understonde, *v.*, understand, gather, 746.

Undertake, *v.*, enter upon an enterprise, 405; 1 *pr. s.*, dare say, affirm, ='believe me,' 288.

Unknowe, unknown, 126.

Untrewe, unfaithfully, untruly, 735.

Usage, practice, custom, 110.

Veine, vein in earth (?), sap vessel, 3.

Venerye, hunting, 166.

Verray, *adj.*, true (NOT *adv.* very), 72.

Vertu, efficacy, (life-giving) power, 4; see note, l. 307.

Vertuous, having manly qualities, morally good, 251.

Viage, voyage, journey, 77.

Vileinye, see THE KNIGHT; **to seye v.,** to say anything shameful or discourteous, 70.

Vitaille, provisions, food, 248.

Voirdit, verdict, decision, 787.

Vouchesauf, *v.*, agree, grant, 812.

Waiteth, *pr. s.*, **w. after,** looks for, expects, 525; *pt. s.*, took precautions, was watchful, 571.

Wan, see **Winne(n).**

War, cautious, prudent, 309; **was w.,** noticed, 157.

War, *pr. s. subj.*, **w. him,** let him beware, 662.

Wastel breed, white, wheaten bread, as opposed to brown bread, or to coarse bread of other grains, for example, for horses, 147.

Watering, watering-place (for horses), 826.

Waterlees, out of the water, 180.

Webbe, weaver, 362.

We(e)l, well, 29; fully, 24; certainly, 256; very, 614.

Weep, see **wepe.**

Wenden, *v.*, go, 21; *pr. pl.*, 16; **wente,** *pt. s.* and 1 *pt. pl.*, 78.

Wepe, *v.*, weep, 144; **wepte,** *pt. s.*, 148.

Wered, *pt. s.*, wore, 75.

Were(n), (1) *pt. pl.*, were, 18; were, *pt. s.* and *pl. subj.*, might (would) be, 68, 81.

Werken, *v.*, act, 779.

Werre, war, 47.

Werte, wart, 555.

Weste, by w., in *or* to the west, 388.

Wette, *pt. s.*, wet, 129.

Wex, wax, 675.

Wey(e), way, 34.

Weyeden, *pt. pl.*, weighed, 454.

Whan, when, 5.

What, why? 184; why! 854; what sort of, 41.

Wheither, whether, 570.

Whelkes, pimples, 632.

Whelpe, young dog, *perhaps* low fellow, 257.

Which, which, what, who, whom, 619; whiche, *pl.*, what sort of people, 40.

Whil, while, 35.

Whilom, once upon a time, formerly, 795.

Wid(e), wide, wide-open, spacious, 28; of wide extent, far-spread, 491.

Widwe, widow, 253.

Wif, woman, wife (married woman), 234; good w., mistress of a household, 445.

Wight, person, 71.

Wimpul, wimple, linen head-dress worn especially by nuns, 151.

Winne, *v.*, win, gain, conquer, 427; wan, *pt. s.*, 442; wonne, *p.p.*, 51.

Winning, profit, 275.

Wis(e), prudent, sensible, having practical ability, skilful, learned, 68; to make it w., to make it a matter of wisdom *or* of much deliberation, 785.

Wisdom, sound judgment, 371; learning, 575.

Wiste, see Woot.

Wit, 'wits,' mind, mental power, 'brains,' 279; my w. is short, I haven't very much brains, 746.

Withalle, in addition, moreover, 127.

Withholde, *p.p.*, retained, maintained (in service), 511.

Withoute(n), without, besides, 343.

Withseye, *v.*, contradict, refuse, 805.

Wo, wretched, cursed, sorrowful, see note, l. 351.

Wodecraft, wood-craft, 110.

Wol, (1) *pr. s.,* will, desire, intend, and as future *auxil.,* 42; 1 *pr. pl.,* 816; **wole,** *pr. s. subj.,* 805; **wolde(n),** *pt. pl.,* 27.

Wonder, wondrously, extremely, 483.

Wonderly, wonderfully, 84.

Wone, custom, wont, 335.

Woning, dwelling, house, 606.

Woninge, *prp.,* living, 388.

Wonne, see Winne.

Wood, mad, 184.

Woot, (1) *pr. s.,* and 2 *pr. pl.,* know, 389; **wiste,** (1) *pt. s.,* 224.

World, fashion (?), see note, ll. 173–176.

Worthy, excellent, distinguished (*esp.* for military skill *or* by position in society), 43 (it is often difficult to distinguish this sense from the following); suitable, having the appropriate *or* suitable qualities (*e.g.* for a steward), 579; (used ironically) 283 (?), 279 (?), 269 (?).

Worthynesse, state of being *worthy,* see **Worthy.**

Wrastlinge, wrestling, 548.

Wrighte, workman, 614.

Write, *v.,* write (with a pen, etc.), 96; **write,** *p.p.,* 161.

Writing, that which is written; action of composing, *e.g.,* a document, 326.

Wroghte, *pt. s.,* acted, 497; **(y)wroght,** *p.p.,* worked, fashioned, 196.

Wrooth, angry, 451.

Y-, If a *p.p.* prefixed by y cannot be found in this section look for the body of the word under the appropriate letter. Thus for ycleped look under **clepen.**

Yaf, see Yeve(n).

Ybore, see Bereth.

Ycome, *p.p.,* come, 77.

Yeddinges, (*probably*) the singing or recitation of romances in verse, 237.

Yeer, *s.* and *pl.,* year(s), 82.

Yeldinge, yield, 596.

Yemanly, in a yeoman-like way, 106.

Yerde, stick, rod, 149.

Yet, yet, nevertheless, 255; as yet, 291; moreover, 612.

Yeve(n), Yive, *v.,* give, 223; **yaf,** *pt. s.,* and *pl.,* 177.

Ygo, *p.p.,* gone, 286, see THE CLERK OF OXFORD.

Yive, see Yeve(n).

Ylad, *p.p.*, led, carried (in cart), 530.
Ylik, like, 592.
Ynogh, enough, plenty, 373.
Yong(e), young, 7.
Yow, you, 73; *dat.*, (to) you, 34.
Ypunisshed, *p.p.*, punished, 657.
Ypurfiled, *p.p.*, trimmed, ornamented at the edge, 193.
Yronne, *p.p.*, run, 8.
Ysene, visible, 592.
Yshorn, *p.p.*, cut, 589.
Yshrive, *p.p.*, shriven, 'confessed,' 226.
Yteyd, *p.p.*, tied, 457.
Ywimpled, *p.p.*, having a wimple, 470.

Zephirus, west wind, 5.